Finding Christ, Finding Life

*How to Live as a Christian
in a Non-Christian World*

D1605742

Von W. Unruh

DISCIPLESHIP RESOURCES

P.O. BOX 840 • NASHVILLE, TENNESSEE 37202-0840

For Peter Paul
Requiescat in pace

ISBN 0-88177-221-6

Library of Congress Catalog Card No. 97-66502

DR221

Contents

Welcome to the Journey

Perhaps you are curious about us Christians and our faith. You don't consider yourself a believer in Jesus, whom we profess as Truth, but you do claim to be a seeker after truth. You want to know what the Christian faith *offers to you* that you can't obtain elsewhere. You also want to know what this faith *expects of you* in return.

Perhaps you have been spiritually restless for some time. You can't quite put your finger on it, and you certainly can't find the words to express what you're feeling. All you know is that you are tired of just *attending* church. You want to start *being* the church.

Perhaps you have just been baptized, or perhaps you are preparing for baptism right now. You don't want to be *mentally informed about* the faith as much as you need *a mentor to form* you in the faith.

Perhaps your pastor, sensitive to the ways you are growing spiritually, has called you to read this book with some other people in your church. And you, trusting your pastor to guide you in the ways of truth, have agreed to do so.

Perhaps you have been a Christian for a long time and have heard everything you are about to read, yet you sense a stirring in your soul. You are ready for Christ to dismantle the clichés you have been living.

If so, this book is for you. In each of the following chapters, we want to take the Christian faith seriously. Instead of repeating easy moralisms that sound trite and lack substance, we are going to seek God's face. Instead of wearing polite smiles that mask our spiritual emptiness, we are going to challenge our cultured assumptions. Instead of pretending that belief in Jesus will somehow protect us against the problems of life, we are going to delve into spiritually weighty matters that tell us truth and teach us to grow in faith.

This will be a difficult task, for nothing in our lives has prepared us for this kind of venture. And yet we are going to do it anyway, for God is with us. As we pray to God and think about Jesus, let us invite the Spirit of God to speak to us. As we read Scripture and share our thoughts with one another, let us learn to practice the disciplines of the church—all over again.

Let us begin.

✠ *December 26, 1996*
The feast day of Saint Stephen First Martyr

1 Repentance

Read: Joel 2:1-2, 12-17; Psalm 51:1-17;
2 Corinthians 5:20b–6:10; Matthew 6:1-6, 16-21

O God, who takes away the sin of the world, speak to us your words of life, that hearing them, we may learn to recognize your voice above the din of our world.

Call us away from our selfish ways that lead to death, and lead us in the way of truth that results in life, that we may be faithful disciples of Jesus Christ, your Son, our Lord, who lives and reigns with you and the Holy Spirit, one God, forever and ever. Amen.

Repentance is not an easy thing to talk about in church these days. Human nature being what it is, though, I suspect that repentance always has been a rather touchy subject. Indeed, talking about repentance makes us fidgety, nervous, uncomfortable; it bothers us. We would almost rather confess to one another how poorly we tithe, which is a very scary thing considering how little we like to talk about our giving patterns! Even to mention the word *repentance* conjures up in our minds images of locust-munching, fire-breathing, pulpit-pounding John the Baptists, of forehead-perspiring fundamentalists and handkerchief-waving television preachers.

If you have had much to do with the church, you have undoubtedly heard plenty of sermons about repentance. I know I have. And depending on the type of church you have attended, you have probably been invited many times to kneel at a mourner's rail to pray.

All the same, were the truth to be told, we often walk away from these sermons unconvinced. We know that repentance is a topic we need to hear and to experience. We may invite God to accomplish this work in our hearts. We may even try to be open to God's Spirit as it seeks to persuade us of the wrong in our lives. And yet we find that our souls are closed to the very idea of repentance. Why?

I think one reason is that the collected wisdom of our culture has taught us that *we cannot really change who we are.* Not knowing any better, we have believed it. Some of these voices have told us we are conditioned by our environment. These voices teach us to say things like, "I can't help what I do. I'm a victim. I come from a dysfunctional family." Others claim our problems can be traced back to our genes. These voices teach us to say things like, "My doctor tells me I'm an alcoholic because I'm genetically predisposed to being an alcoholic."

Still other voices offer us a second reason when they tell us *we cannot change what we have done.* We are a bound people, marked forever by the things we did yesterday. These voices teach us to say, "Once a liar, always a liar!" "You stole once; you will steal again." "You made your bed. Now you must lie in it." Over and over again, until we learn to believe it ourselves, our culture tells us we cannot escape who we have been or what we have done. But this is not true.

God frees us of our bondage to sin

So, what is true? We know we have not lived as we should. Time and again we have chosen our ways over God's ways and embarrassed God's body—the church. Perhaps we have even led people astray, away from God. I know I've done wrong. And so have you. Indeed, the more I realize how much I have hurt people (not to mention the times I have hurt God), the more amazed I am that God continues to take an active interest in me.

Because I know that all this is true, there are times when life over-whelms me and I grow frustrated. And once I am convinced that I can escape neither my heritage nor my yesterdays, I begin to lose hope! For there is nothing I can do to relieve my growing sense of guilt and shame. Like Paul long ago, I cry in agony that the good I want to do I can't, but nei-ther can I avoid the evil I don't want to do (Romans 7:14-24).

Frustrated by our inability to change, embarrassed by our growing assortment of crimes committed, sooner or later we helplessly cry out for help. And the same culture that has convinced us that we cannot change is now quite ready to teach us how to live with ourselves. Unfortunately, what it teaches us is how to practice the fine art of denial. Legally, we are taught to look for loopholes. Psychologically, we are taught to blame others for our failings. Like father Adam and mother Eve, we try to excuse our actions by holding others more responsible than ourselves (Genesis 3:11-13).

This, however, is not the way Christ invites us to live. Neither is it the way we Christians believe. We rightly despair of ever being able to fix our-selves. But blaming others for our problems will not solve our problems. Indeed, in time it will only make matters worse. What, then, can we do? Where, then, can we turn? Is there hope for a people like us?

Yes, there is; but it is a costly way that means learning a new way of handling the issues we face in life. It is a way that requires us to turn to God for the help we cannot offer ourselves, for God alone can do for us the things we find it impossible to do for ourselves (Mark 10:27). In fact, God has already! In the life, death, and resurrection of Jesus, God has already broken the stranglehold with which the sins of yesterday have tried their best to bind us. To a people crying for help, surely this news is good news, which is why the church insists on calling this news *gospel*.

This insight brings two important points into focus. First, repentance is not something we can achieve by trying harder to do what is right. Our repentance is always a result of God's grace. So right from the start, and this is the second point, discussions about our repentance should always emphasize God's mercy, not our depraved state. For what ultimately matters is not what we have done or said or been or caused. It is not the extent of our sin that is important. The only thing that matters is the depth of God's love.

In practical terms, this means that the church's invitation to repentance ought finally to fill us with hope and joy, not burden us with guilt and frustration. Why? Because this is a way that brings to us the hope and comfort and release from bondage that we have been seeking all along. But invitations to repentance will not accomplish their objective if all they do is make us feel lousy about ourselves. For these calls to repentance to be meaningful, they need to do much more than cause us to experience guilt. To be sure, in our shameless world we probably need to experience some guilt. But ultimately, calls to repentance need to reveal to us God's estimation of our worth, for they are a heaven-sent revelation that initially will surprise us, then shame us, and finally sanctify us.

God's forgiveness precedes our repentance

Again and again in Scripture, we are invited to repent of our wrong *doing* and of our wrong *thinking* and to seek God. John the Baptist, eyes blazing, stood beside the Jordan River and yelled at those milling about him, "Repent, for the kingdom of heaven has come near" (Matthew 3:2). In time, Jesus repeated this message by saying to all who would listen, "The kingdom of God has come near; repent" (Mark 1:15). As the disciples poured out of the upper room on Pentecost morning, Peter remembered his Lord's counsel and offered it to those who asked for spiritual direction, "Repent, and be baptized" (Acts 2:38).

These disciples, and the countless men and women who have followed in their steps, were not angry people filled with spite, preaching a gospel of hatred and bitterness. They were people whose hearts had been touched by the redeeming love of God. Their call to repentance was not an angry attack on people they viewed as their spiritual inferiors. It was a loving invitation to share the wondrous joy of God's mercy. Having received

God's loving forgiveness themselves, they wanted others to share the experience, too.

Our repentance is always a result of God sharing grace with us. This is a point that bears repeating, for sometimes even church folk are guilty of taking God's grace for granted. It happens when we tell people that if they want to join our church, they will need to straighten up first. It happens when we make it sound as if God will not love us until we "get saved." Thankfully, these comments are not true. The psalmist said that God "does not deal with us according to our sins, nor repay us according to our iniquities" (Psalm 103:8-10). And Paul added that God loved us while we were yet bound by our sin (Romans 5:8).

We sometimes talk as if our words of repentance trigger some kind of chemical reaction in God that requires God to forgive us. Some people even think that when they decide they want to become a Christian, all they have to do is say, "Okay, God. I'm ready now." But that is not the way our repentance and God's forgiveness work. We are not the ones who initiate this spiritual process by reciting a mantra to which God has no choice but to react favorably. No, we are the respondents—always. To put it rather bluntly, *God's forgiveness is not contingent on our repentance* (John 3:16). Rather, our repentance is contingent on God's forgiveness. Thank goodness, then, that God's forgiveness precedes not only our acts of repentance but also our sin. Indeed, God forgave us nearly two thousand years ago at the very time Jesus, God's Son, was gasping for breath, dangling naked from a tree on which we had pinned him.

Contrary to the claims of our culture, we can change, but only because God has forgiven us already. We are not compelled by our environment to act in certain ways. We are not restricted by our gene pool. We are not bound by our sin. And we do not have to cover our sin by blaming others for our failings. Instead, we can turn to God for help, for God is always more ready to give than we are to receive. With God's help, we can admit we have been wrong. We can confess our sin openly. We can promise to live in imitation of God. All this is the work and result of God's grace in our lives.

Of course, our world is apt to scoff at this work. For our world believes that admission of guilt is a sign of weakness, that the only reason to make promises is to buy the time needed to make one's position more secure. Our world laughs at our confession of sin as a mark of naiveté, proof that we cannot handle the harsh realities of life. And we would have to admit that love and trust and good faith do not make much sense within the systems that tend to prevail in our fallen world. All they do is leave us terribly vulnerable, which is precisely where they intended to leave us all along!

In God's world, which we claim this one is, where death must finally succumb to life and where darkness finds it impossible to extinguish light, there is another power at work. In God's world, love conquers power, and trust overcomes faithlessness—every time. Rather than loving us conditionally or rewarding us only when we have responded properly, God simply loves us from the beginning, fully convinced that that love alone has the power to recall our prodigal hearts. And you know what? God is right!

This is good news! This is the heart of the gospel! This is what Joel wanted the people to gather around him to hear. It is why he wanted to call a solemn assembly in the first place! For this is a message our world needs to hear. It is a word that needs to touch our wounded world's hard heart. It is a word that needs to pierce our own hearts. As Paul said, "Don't you see? Now is the acceptable time; now is the day of salvation!" We don't have to wait for tomorrow to receive God's forgiveness or to express our repentance. We don't have to continue weeping over the burdens our yesterdays have imposed upon us. We don't have to muck around in the guilt of past sin. We don't even have to worry about what sorry trick our gene pool is going to pull on us this time. For God has forgiven us already. Fully! All those things that have clouded our vision, upset our judgment, or mocked our good name can be let go of. Because God loves us, we are a forgiven people!

Repentance is more than confession

Being released from the bondage of our sins is the first step in what we are calling a life of repentance. It is an act of trust in God's character, of belief in God's word, of acceptance of God's forgiveness. It is the first of many responses we can now make to God in thanksgiving for all that God has done for us. Our repentant acceptance of God's mercy becomes the first note of a life of praise that we can begin to sing to the glory of God. From this moment on, every act we accomplish, every word we speak, every thought we think can become a grace-prompted thank-you or a glorious shout of praise to God.

Let me express a note of caution, though. We tend to confuse confession and repentance and to think that because we have done the one, we have done the other as well. This is not so. Confession is our admission that we have either done wrong or been wrong. When we confess, we take responsibility for our wrong actions. We stop excusing ourselves or blaming others for our wrong. As important as confession is, though, it is but the prelude to repentance. True repentance can occur only after we accept God's forgiveness. With the power of God's Spirit at work in our lives, God begins to re-create us. Released from the sterile grip of death in which we have lived for so long, we begin to change into new people. Along with our new lease on life comes the blessing of hope and the assurance of love and the gifts of joy and peace. Adopted into God's family, we are freed to live life a new way. We can begin to live it God's way.

In other words, confession is the vital prelude to repentance. This is why we are invited in worship on Sunday mornings to confess our sin to God and to one another. But notice that, having confronted us with the gravity of our sin, our pastor immediately assumes the role of priest and absolves us of our guilt by reminding us that God loves us and has for-given us already. Otherwise, we would be left standing before God as naked sinners, and that is not a particularly comfortable place to stand. The church speaks of sin, not to condemn us or to judge us as spiritually unfit, but to open our ears that we might hear God's words of forgiveness spoken. In turn, we hear the gospel as good news, not because it tells us we are sinners, but because it tells us God has overcome our sin. We speak of sin only to be done with it!

Repentance ushers in a new way of life

Lest we draw a wrong conclusion, though, let me hasten to add that repentance is never something we do once and are then done with for-ever. The act that makes our repentance possible cost God the life of the Son. Were our response a lone, solitary response, it could never speak an adequate word of thanks to God. Thanks be to God, then, that we, freed from our past and forgiven for our sin, can begin to live daily in new ways that honor God and bless Jesus. No longer bound by our culture's wrong opinions, we can rely on the power of God's Spirit to produce in us acts and words and thoughts that teach us to be generous like God.

What, then, are the forms that repentance takes in our lives? Jesus sug-gested that as our newfound freedom takes root and matures, it expresses itself in loving acts of generosity like the giving of alms, prayer, and fast-ing. Since we are not used to spiritual disciplines like these, we may won-der how these archaic-sounding acts can possibly express an attitude of repentance or foster a lifestyle of holiness. But Jesus was convinced that these three acts are sacramental in the way they convey God's grace, and merciful in the way they express our humble love. They are the fruit of our repentance.

Consider the way we handle our money—our giving of alms. Afraid of what tomorrow may bring, bound by selfish concerns rooted in yesterday, our world hoards its money unnecessarily and spends it frivolously. But freed of these culturally-based fears, Christians learn to share money the way God shares grace. Jesus suggested that our giving of alms is one of the ways that we can make our repentance real and can live in imitation of God. Contrary to what we may think, the church does not take up a collection in worship simply to pay its bills. The church collects money to teach us to be generous like Jesus, to give us the opportunity to practice our repentance in a community of grace. As we learn to give alms in worship, we root our repentance in the soil of God's love. In time, we learn to give alms outside of worship, too. Indeed, the more generous we become with our money, the more generous we become with our lives, and the more complete our repentance grows. The alternative is to remain stingy with our money. But the more stingy we remain with our lives, the less repentant our spirits can grow. Only by giving alms can we break the cycles of stinginess we have been taught by our culture and learn to live our repentance daily in deep thanks to God.

Consider the way we handle our time—our participation in prayer. Convinced that it must look after itself, our world works long hours, endures long lines, and suffers long commutes in relative isolation. But freed of these shackles of convenience that waste our time, we finally begin to have the time to share, both with others and with God. In prayer, we can talk to God or listen. We can ponder God's will or reflect upon God's goodness. We can even simply choose to spend time with God, doing nothing particularly special at all. As we learn to spend our time with God, we learn how to spend our time with others, too; for prayer grounds our repentance in the reality of God. It enables us to acknowledge that our time is not our own, that our lives are not our own. Only by praying constantly can we reclaim our time and learn to live our repentance daily in the holy presence of God.

Consider the way we juggle our priorities—our attempt to fast spiritually. Concerned only about itself, our culture teaches us that greed is respectable. Bound by a spirit of gluttony, we learn to overfill our homes with things and our bodies with food. Periodically embarrassed by the bulges, though, we haul our overflowing closets to charitable organizations and enroll our unsightly bodies in crash diets, all to no avail. But freed of our bondage to this repetitious cycle of consumption, we can learn to simplify our lives by hungering and thirsting after the righteousness of God. For fasting is not the religious equivalent of some ancient diet ritual. It is not the way Christians control weight problems. In fact, it has nothing to do with how pear-shaped our bodies may or may not be. Fasting is a sign of our repentance, a mark of our increasingly great hunger for God, a sign of our willingness to ignore the growl in our stomachs in order to satisfy the spiritual longing in our souls. This is not nearly as crazy as it may sound. Surely we have missed meals to meet deadlines at work. We couldn't do this all the time, of course; but the more like Jesus we become, the more willing we are to sacrifice our priorities to heed the priorities of God. Fasting is an act that plants our repentance in the mercy of God. It leads to lifestyles of simplicity that reveal to our world that daily we are becoming more humble and generous, just like God, whose love of us has made our love possible.

Conclusion

In this life, death lurks all around us. Every day, in all sorts of ways, it tries to lay its cold hands on us. Through the words and acts and attitudes of our culture, it silences our hopes and throttles our love. But there is another way to live. It is the way of Jesus, who offered up his life for us to remind us that our struggle against death is a battle *he wages for us* every moment of our repentant lives. The loving result of his blessed death is that death holds no more sting for Christians who live our repentance faithfully. Indeed, every act of repentance we perform is a sharing in Jesus' victory over death, even our ordinary acts like the giving of alms and the offering of prayers and the undergoing of fasts. Through these acts we reach for God. By these acts we express our desire to be like God. They are the form Jesus says our repentance can now take, this day and all days.

Thanks be to God!

We confess, O God, that we have not been a repentant people. Hemmed in by guilt and frustrated by feelings of hopelessness, we have looked after ourselves rather than care for your people. Instead of giving generously, we have hoarded our possessions and sought higher pay. Instead of praying intently, we have lived without purpose and collapsed nightly in pointless fatigue. Instead of fasting spiritually, we have eaten on the run and satisfied only our stomachs.

Forgive us, we pray, for choosing our ways apart from your way. Close our ears to the whispers of our world. Absolve our guilt and form us in your image. Accept our offerings and encourage our repentance. Teach us to show forth your glory in all our acts. Lord, in your mercy, hear our prayer.

2 Temptation

Read: Deuteronomy 26:1-11; Psalm 91:1-2, 9-16;
Romans 10:8b-13; Luke 4:1-13

O God, who offers your people the consolation of the Spirit, protect us when temptation tries to ensnare us, that we may stand firm in our faith in you.
Guard us against the tendency to exchange our faithfulness to your Word for an analysis of your words, that we may ever serve you, and love and honor Jesus Christ, your Son, our Lord, who lives and reigns with you and the Holy Spirit, one God, forever and ever. Amen.

Sooner or later, we all have to come to terms with who we are. What does it mean that we are a repentant people, the children of God, created in love and re-created for glory? The question arises out of the depths of the gospel. It also suggests to us where our faith journey is taking us. As we mature into the likeness of Jesus, we are not to become showy hypocrites but faithful sons and daughters led by the Spirit. When we give alms, we are not to judge the worth of the other. Instead, we are to refuse to let our right hand know what our left is doing. When we offer prayers, we are not to babble as the pagans do, hoping to manipulate God by our fine words; we are to trust God to supply our need. When we fast, we are not to perform our spiritual acts to draw attention to our holy ways; we are to focus our thoughts on God alone.

Coming to terms with who we are means coming to terms with God's call on our lives. By this call, God intends to lead us away from our sin-filled past. And God does. But sooner or later, this call will take us down a path that reaches what seems to be an impasse—an impasse not unlike that faced by the people of Israel. Pursued by the Egyptians, the Israelites were running headlong toward the Red Sea. What's more, God seemed to be leading them into the Sea! So we, pursued by the hostile world of our own Egypt—our culture—that is not pleased with who we are becoming, will be forced to make a decision. Should we trust more in the mercy of Egypt advancing or in the love of God beckoning?

Here is where we learn that physical appearances can be spiritually deceiving. What we see is not always what we get. For Egypt is not pursuing us to rescue us, and neither is our Lord leading us to the water's edge merely to abandon us. For Christians, there is always a path that lies straight ahead, straight through the water. We may be unable to see it at first. We may not believe that it is there. But when we finally still our cries for help, our ears will detect a familiar voice calling to us. It is the voice of our faithful Lord, inviting us to do what does not seem possible, inviting us to enter the waters. With nowhere else to go, and without understanding why entering the waters is necessary or how it is possible or even what might result, we wade on in. In response to our Lord's call, we enter the waters and feel them part beneath us in a swirling acceptance of us.

Once we are safe on the far side, we offer to God our heart-felt praise with jubilant thanks. Delighted that the way of faith seems so easy, wondering why we didn't do this years before, we are apt to grow spiritually cocky. So it is that, hardly out of the water, we hear again the familiar voice wooing us on, reminding us that our journey is far from complete. This time, we notice that the path is heading for what looks like wilderness. It is a path we find tough to tread, for the wilderness is a murky, dense, uninhabitable sort of place, full of the shadowy haunts and filthy recesses of temptation. Given the choice, we would prefer that our faith result in a life of ease and plenty. But when it comes to issues of faith, there are no choices to make. There are only calls to accept.

Thankfully, we are not the first people to have to come to terms with who we are. This is, after all, the same path Israel had to tread as they left Egypt behind. It is the same journey Jesus had to take, too. Thankfully, the temptations we meet in the wilderness are not unique, either. Evil is hopelessly unimaginative. The temptations we face in this life are the same ones Jesus faced in the wilderness, the same ones Israel experienced before him.

We will face temptation in this life

We do young Christians a disservice when we tell them the Christian walk is a life of ease, the answer to all their problems. That is not the kind of promise our Lord makes. It is the kind of promise our world makes. In truth, the repentant life is not easy. It is a constant struggle against the wiles of the devil, a pruning away from us of all that is unproductive and unfaithful, a constant dying to self and rising again to new life. It is an uncomfortable time that strains our new faith before it consoles our terrified spirits.

This is not to say that the repentant life is not a life of joy, for it is. This is simply to be honest about the new life Christians are given. Living as a Christian in a world that is not particularly fond of Christ's presence in our lives is not easy. To survive the taunts of our world and the temptations of the devil, our trust in God must become as tempered as steel, our powers of spiritual discernment honed to a fine edge. To this end, faith must be formed in us. For we are not born faithful; we must be made faithful.

To accomplish this work in the souls who heed God's call, the Spirit of God leads us into the desert. Moses spent forty years here. Paul stayed fourteen years. Jesus was here forty days. Here our haughty spirits are reproved, re-formed by the humility of Jesus. Here our impatient attitudes are confronted by the long-suffering mercy of God. Here our cantankerous ways are overcome by the compassion of God's Holy Spirit. Here we are given the time and space necessary to sort out our priorities as we learn to live our new convictions.

God's leading us into the desert may seem cruel and unloving of God. It may sound very unlike something the Spirit of God would do. But there is only one way to get from bondage in Egypt-land to residence in promised Canaan-land. The journey leads inevitably through the desert. This is as true spiritually for us today as it was physically for Israel yesterday. Only in the wilderness will we develop the skills necessary to tell the difference between the truth of God and the promises of this world.

Even though chances are quite good that the devil will take advantage of the situation, it remains a gracious and loving thing for the Spirit to lead us repentant, baptized followers of Jesus into the desert. For, as Paul said, no matter where we are, even apparently all alone in the desert, God has promised us that we will not be tempted beyond what we are able to bear (1 Corinthians 10:13). This is a promise that we must learn for ourselves is sure, and the only way to do that is to trust actively in the One who first made the promise. But in time, we discover in our dependence upon God that God's Spirit acts as a breastplate of righteousness in our lives, quenching all the fiery darts the devil tosses our way (Ephesians 6:10-17).

Temptation is not sin

Before we go any further, there are some misunderstandings about the relationship between temptation and sin that we need to address. When we give our lives to Jesus and become Christians, our lives immediately begin to change; for the power and love of God begin to course through us. Where once we were full of ourselves and did everything for ourselves, now we become a repentant people. We learn to let go of ourselves and trust in God. Old patterns of life get sloughed off. Old habits cease to rule. Our lips speak forth God's praise. Set aside for God and made holy by God, we start looking and acting like God. We are made new creatures (2 Corinthians 5:17), and outward sin comes to an end.

But sin is subtle. While its most visible expressions are removed quickly from our lives, all the inward expressions of sin that show up in our attitudes against others and congeal into a hardness of heart against God generally take a lifetime of committed struggle against the world to overcome. This struggle is the journey that the church calls growth in grace, sanctification, Christian maturity. But learning obedience renders us spiritually exhausted, and seeking God's face and striving to come to terms with our calling leaves us more susceptible than ever before to the wiles of the devil.

If you have never focused your attention solely on God, this susceptibility to the ways of the devil may come as a surprise. We tend to assume that the more we seek God's face, the less temptation will bother us. In reality the exact opposite occurs. We never know the truly seductive power of evil until we offer to God the gift of our repentance and receive from God the gift of God's Spirit. Only then do the temptations of the devil become uncomfortably real and fill us with anguish. The more deliberately we seek God, the more demonically difficult and devilishly daring temptation becomes. The more deliberately we study Scripture and offer our prayers and give our alms, the more tempted we are to expect God to treat us with special favor.

There are three things, then, that we should note carefully. First, the presence of the Holy Spirit in our lives does not keep temptation from happening. Indeed, we don't really begin to experience tough temptation until after we are filled with the Spirit. The Spirit does not protect us from having to face the devil's temptations, but the Spirit does share with us the power of God so that we are able to withstand them as they occur.

Second, even though Jesus had no sin in his life, he was as prone to temptation as we are (Hebrews 4:15). Indeed, the devil ran every test it could think of on Jesus and made still other plans to come back later. That is a word of gospel to us! For the presence of temptation in our lives is neither a sign of guilt nor a result of sin. It is only a devilish invitation to sin.

Third, as a truly human being, Jesus had no special resources at his disposal to overcome his temptations other than those we have. He had to emerge victorious over his temptations the same way we do over ours. Just like us, he had to rely fully on the grace and power of God present in the Holy Spirit, witnessed to in Holy Scripture, lived out in communities of faith. Because he overcame temptation, we believe we can, too!

Temptation challenges our identities

As was the case with Jesus, most temptations that we Christians face in life do not blatantly invite us to violate the Ten Commandments. While the thought may flit through our minds, most of us are not tempted to stab someone in the back or steal a car or engage in open promiscuity. Temptations are much more subtle than that. Rather than attack us through questionable *activities*, they confront us by questioning our *identities*. They tempt us to let go of our faith. Only then do they encourage us to make stones into bread, to sell our souls to the devil in exchange for spiritual victories, to test the Lord in provocative ways.

Like us, like Israel before him, Jesus too had to come to terms with his identity. At his baptism, he had heard God say to him, "You are my Son, the Beloved; with you I am well pleased" (Luke 3:22). It was this identity that the devil called into question in the wilderness. "So, you are the Son of God," mused the devil in Jesus' ear. This old and extremely subtle but highly effective trick takes our focus off of God and places it squarely on us. The serpent in the garden used it against Adam and Eve. We have heard the whispers in our ears, too. "So, God loves you. You must be someone very special! You must be one of the privileged ones. But tell me, then, why is one of God's privileged ones suffering so? Surely God doesn't desire this for you! If you are one of God's privileged ones, ask God to help you! Tell God to take away this hurt!"

That doesn't sound like much of a temptation, does it? Indeed, it sounds like what we have been told and what we have come to believe is the very substance of the gospel itself. We are told that we are children of God. God loves us. God doesn't want us to suffer. God doesn't expect us to go hungry. If we have no money, if we need a new job, if we can't handle the pressure, if we can't find a parking place, we are told to remind God of God's promises and to believe in faith that God will give it to us. We are to expect it to be done, for we are the children of God. But beware! Regardless of what some may say, this is not the *faith* of Christ. This is the *temptation* of Christ!

Upon entering the desert, Jesus expected to deepen his spirituality by engaging in a variety of spiritual exercises including prayer and fasting, two of the three acts by which we make our repentance real. For forty days Jesus had held a religious fast and sought God's will and learned to depend upon God alone. As each of the forty days in the desert passed, Jesus became increasingly dependent upon God. He also became increasingly hungry. Toward the end of those forty days, the tempter suggested a rather common-sense solution to Jesus' hunger, given the abilities Jesus supposedly had: "If you are the Son of God, tell this stone to become bread."

Well, there is nothing in Scripture that says, "Thou shalt not turn stones into bread." But that is what makes temptation so dangerously deceptive. Rarely are temptations brazenly anti-scriptural. Rather, they challenge our identity as children of God. They raise doubts about our relationship with God. Just before entering the desert, Jesus had been told, "You are my Son." Now the devil was raising the intriguing question, "I don't mean to be disrespectful, Jesus, but if you are God's Son, what are you doing out here in the middle of nowhere starving? Make some food! Eat!" It sounds rather like what the devil whispered in the garden of Eden, doesn't it? "Did God really say you are the Son of God, Jesus?" said the devil. "If he did, don't you think you should probably find out for sure out here in private before you make a fool of yourself in public?"

Temptation challenges our activities

After they question the *reality* of our identities, temptations then invite us to *take advantage* of our identities. "Jesus," said the devil, "excuse me for asking, but what good is your Sonship going to do anybody if you starve to death out here in the middle of nowhere? Shouldn't you be doing something constructive? Are you sure you understood what God was asking you to do? Shouldn't you use this time to learn how to take advantage of your identity? Shouldn't you use this identity in powerfully righteous ways? Why don't you fill the needs of the people you meet?"

Lured by shortcuts that promise to ease our struggle while pointing to God's goodness, we are tempted to test the extent of God's love. Rather than invite God's will to be done in our lives, we are urged to issue our own ultimatums, to demand that our will be accepted by God. In the end, though, every temptation is an all-or-nothing affair that invites us to justify the means we are using by the ends we hope to accomplish. "Worship me," says the devil. "I will give you all these things you want, including the things you need, for an awfully lot less than will your God." Indeed, at its core, temptation is always an enticement to lose patience, to lose nerve, to set aside our trust in God's way. It is an invitation to create for ourselves a new god that will make the same promises but at much less cost to us.

Under the guise of offering Jesus what he needed, the devil threatened to snare Christ's soul. And Jesus felt the pull of that offer, just as you and I do. What could it hurt! Who could it hurt! The rocks were abundant, and there was no denying that Jesus' need was real. It may sound innocent enough, but the inducement to use our spiritual identity for personal gain is always a demonic temptation to choose evil and spurn God. There are no exceptions! God does not exist to serve us. We exist to serve God. God does not bow at our feet like a conjured-up genie and call us Lord, treating our wishes like his commands. We bow before God, whom we call Lord. Our identity as the sons and daughters of God doesn't grant us the right to demand privileges from God. Rather, it is a gracious sign that we are becoming like God.

"But that's just too subtle," you say. "I'm no saint. I'm no scholar, either. If the distinctions between temptation and righteousness are that fine, I might as well throw in the towel, for I haven't the insight necessary to discern that kind of difference." You are right, of course. You don't have that insight. But then, I wasn't born with that spiritual tool, either. Neither was Jesus. Discerning right from wrong is not a birthright we possess. It is a gift the Spirit shares with us in ample abundance, an ability we can hone by prayer and study. Had Jesus not allowed Holy Scripture to fill his mind and judge his soul, he would never have had available to him the spiritual resources he needed to overcome the devil's tempting offer. Neither will we. Prayer, study, and training are not options available only for the spiritually elite. They are the fundamental building blocks for all who would become disciples of Jesus. They establish our faith. We make time for them in order to live. We ignore them to our own spiritual demise. Temptation never has been child's play. It is always a matter of life and death, and it is our souls that hang in the balance.

Temptation is so difficult to see through because it seems to pit the *work* of God against the *word* of God. Given a different set of circumstances, the devil's temptation of Jesus could have been divine instruction. Hungry and exhausted, Jesus was tempted to think that if God truly loved him, God should be taking care of him. But the longer Jesus pondered the idea, the more fully he realized that God had been taking care of him all along and would certainly continue to take care of him. Only as he reflected on the words of the tempter in light of his present situation did Jesus understand that he was being asked to exploit the privilege of Sonship he enjoyed. Only then did he grasp for sure how wrong the words of the devil were. Only then did he realize that this wasn't the voice he had learned to recognize in Scripture, for that voice had said that we don't live by bread alone but by the words God feeds us. God had sustained him now for forty days. Who was Jesus to wrest matters into his own hands?

Conclusion

Jesus was doing exactly what God had asked him to do. Led by the Spirit, he was in the desert learning obedience. His hunger was not the result of inhuman poverty; it was self-inflicted, part of a spiritual discipline. He was doing it because God had told him to do it. He believed that it would enable him to draw closer to God. And the devil's temptation challenged his identity precisely at the level of that spiritual discipline.

It is at this stage in our spiritual maturity that we are so very vulnerable ourselves. Led into the desert like all young Christians are, we strive to take seriously God's call upon our lives. We meet for worship. We celebrate Holy Communion. We study Scripture. We have fellowship with one another. Joy pervades all we do. We give alms. We pray. We fast. And in the state of human dependency these acts create, a state that bonds our lives to the life of Jesus, suddenly we hear the evil whispers deep in the recesses of our own being. "Are you sure you know what you are doing? Are you sure this pain is worth it? Are you sure this is what Jesus told you to do? What are you hoping to accomplish by this? Since when does Jesus make you hurt? Since when does Jesus deny you? I thought Jesus was supposed to fulfill you!"

We didn't ask God to put us out here in the desert to learn obedience. But here we are, all the same; and the surroundings are pretty barren. There's not much to do but pray and fast. And daily we are having stripped from us all those things we have learned to depend upon. Out here it's just God and us, and all these strange visions and demonic temptations. God knows we are new at this. We don't know what to do next. We are not even sure we know what God's voice sounds like. All we know is that this is where God has brought us; and where God leads us, there we have said we will follow, all the way. So here we are, wondering why so many of our dreams come to nothing, why our hopes and aspirations have to wither and die. We are awaiting further instructions, faithfully practicing the disciplines, trying our best to be brave, and hoping against hope that we will be mature enough to recognize the right signs when they appear. With God's help we will, you know! For strange as it may seem, this barren place is exactly where God wants us to be right now.

God help us all! And for this help, thanks be to God!

We confess, O God, that because we find your way hard, we resist your Spirit's wilderness call. We want to do your will; but when it conflicts with our happiness, we waver. We are weak, and the temptations we face seem so strong, even though you promise they are not. Because our faith is small, we trust in our own strength, not in your love. Because our faith is immature, we demand your compliance to our desires. We are still so apt to test your love and question your covenant.

Forgive us, we pray, for not trusting you more fully. Strengthen our weak wills by teaching us the promises of Scripture. Disperse our great doubt by leading us faithfully. Reject our impatient demands for immediate fulfillment by reminding us of the divine mercy we'd forfeit. Lord, in your mercy, hear our prayer.

3 Covenant

Read: Genesis 15:1-12, 17-18; Psalm 27;
Philippians 3:17–4:1; Luke 13:31-35

O God, who is not willing that any should perish, but who wills that all may have eternal life, share with us your mercy, that we may learn to share with you our love.

Make us a righteous people who seek your face and trust your word and love your Spirit, that we may keep the covenant you offer us in Jesus Christ, your Son, our Lord, who lives and reigns with you and the Holy Spirit, one God, in glory everlasting. Amen.

Christians don't like their faith to be tested any more than anyone else does, but temptation is simply a part of life. Because we live in a fallen world, we can't avoid it. No matter how spiritually mature we may become, we will be confronted with a variety of temptations that pit our spiritual resources against the cumulative sin that pervades our world. To the degree that we rely upon God to guide us through these thickets, we are destined to emerge a pruned but holy people. In the end we will be more certain of our God's great love and less enamored with a world that has lost its soul and is trying desperately to make us lose ours. Both our faith and our experience have taught us, though, that if we try to fight these skirmishes of faith apart from God, we don't have a prayer. As Martin Luther grasped so clearly some five hundred years ago, "Did we in our own strength confide, our striving would be losing" ("A Mighty Fortress Is Our God," *The United Methodist Hymnal;* The United Methodist Publishing House, 1992; 110).

Let's be clear about this, though. Were desert temptations the only spiritual dilemma that Christians faced, life would not be so bad. For even though temptation is a devilish nuisance, a bothersome problem that tries to divert our attention away from God, the good news is that we can overcome it in Christ! But there are other struggles we face regularly in our relationship with God, and they can be just as debilitating. The worst of these occurs when, all alone in the desert and hounded by hell, we start to wonder if God is keeping God's end of this bargain we struck in good faith. We begin to doubt God. It is a harrowing struggle that we Christians would not have to face if we did not respond to God's call so fully.

But that's just it. Having accepted God's forgiveness, we have responded with our repentance. We have turned away from the bondage of our past and received from God an incredible spiritual freedom that has transformed our lives by freeing our souls. Initially frightened when the temptations of our world reared their head in earnest, we have learned to fight back by trusting in God alone. As God's Spirit helps us overcome these temptations, our spirits are buoyed by grace and filled with divine passion. We know our lives are secure in God's hands. In the rapturous joy that accompanies these moments, we are convinced that heaven has drawn near. Without hesitation we have given our future over to God and said to God with all the love of an adopted son or daughter of faith, "Your will be done with my life!"

But then, with little or no warning whatsoever, clouds of doubt begin to roll in, obscuring our vision of God and darkening the counsel of God. A night of spiritual darkness begins to envelop us. We are confused and distraught. For at the very same time that the questions fill our minds and the doubts invade our spirits, God seems to have grown uncharacteristically silent, unresponsive to our cries.

Remaining faithful when God seems unresponsive

If you have reached this crossroad in your journey, you know it is not a pleasant phenomenon to experience. The spiritual struggle that ensues when doubt creeps in and fills the cavities of our souls is terribly disorienting. For this is not a temptation that challenges *our* identities. This temptation is more audacious. It encourages us to challenge *God's* identity at precisely those times when God seems farthest away and most unresponsive to us.

God has promised us in Scripture that if we ask, it will be given us; that if we seek, we will find; that if we knock, it will be opened to us (Matthew 7:7-8). Why, then, are there times when we ask with all the faith we can muster, but God gives us nothing? Why are there times when we seek God's will diligently but find nothing we recognize? Why are there times when we knock loudly and persistently, but no doors open to us anywhere? Had we engaged in some willful sin for which God had need to punish us, we could perhaps understand. But we haven't. Besides, one of the truths we learn as we serve our Lord is that there is nothing we can do —or fail to do—to lessen God's love of us. So, our bewilderment deepens.

Here we must confront another of those subtle but pervasive myths of our culture that has made its way into the very fabric of the church's proclamation. Contrary to what we are told is the gospel truth, nowhere in Scripture do we Christians read that one of our life goals should be our self-fulfillment or our self-realization. God never encourages us to "be all that we can be." Rather, we are invited to deny ourselves and to follow in the footsteps of Christ. We are expected to take up our cross daily and to follow Jesus alone (Luke 9:23). As the old catechisms insisted, the chief end of us human beings is to glorify God (*The Westminster Shorter Catechism*).

In his own faith journey, Abraham had to come to terms with the fact that serving God is not the same thing as feeling self-fulfilled. We, too, must come to terms with this spiritual truth. Indeed, it was because he thought the church was forgetting that God has called us to be servants of Christ that John Wesley strived to remind us, "Christ has many services to be done. Some are more easy and honorable, others are more difficult and disgraceful. Some are suitable to our inclinations and interests, *others are contrary to both.* In some we may please Christ and please ourselves. *But then there are other works where we cannot please Christ except by denying ourselves.* It is necessary, therefore, that we consider what it means to be a servant of Christ" ("Wesley's Covenant Service," *The United Methodist Book of Worship;* ©1992 The United Methodist Publishing House; Used by permission; Italics added; page 291).

This path of servanthood is a path that all God's people must travel. Take Abraham, for instance. For some fifteen years he had struggled to make sense of God's call to leave his home in Ur of the Chaldeans. He was quite sure that God had promised him two things: a son and land. Neither promise had as yet come true. He had no son. He had no land. And he was now ninety years old. Too old to believe in fairy tales any longer, he was rapidly approaching that age when clinging to unreasonable beliefs is a sign that your mind is not as clear as it should be. So, when Abraham received another vision in a fitful sleep one afternoon, he questioned God's voice openly: "Lord, you know I have tried to be faithful to you. I have gone where you have led me. I have done as you have bid me. I have believed as you have spoken to me. Why, then, are you mocking me? You know I have no children, Lord! Have I somehow misunderstood you?"

God said, "I am not mocking you, Abraham. And no, you have not misunderstood me. You will have a son. Indeed, in time your children will be as numerous as the stars in the night sky. Trust me."

Well, that's the rub, isn't it! Our trust is the one thing we are not prepared to give without some proof that God is going to follow through on God's end of the bargain. Yet despite the fact that Abraham felt that God was being exceptionally slow in keeping God's promises, Scripture tells us that Abraham chose to believe that the Lord was a faithful God. And God bore witness in his own Spirit that Abraham was indeed a righteous man.

Recognizing doubt as a prelude to self-interest

To be sure, it is one thing simply to *assert* with Abraham that trust is the antidote to our doubt. It is quite another actually to *live* it. How are we to account for this sudden influx of doubt? More important, how do we overcome it? How do we sustain faith when spiritual anxiety floods our souls? How are we to respond when we discover that other Christians are not as perfect as they profess to be? What are we to think when our prayers remain unanswered, or when our faithful service lies unrewarded or unrecognized? How do we maintain hope when our hope is deferred time and again? How do we persevere in times that are dark and when life makes no sense at all?

The only way to overcome our doubt of God is to cling even more tightly to the God we want to trust in. You see, the kind of doubt that we experience as spiritual anxiety is not sin, though it can certainly *become* sinful. It is a normal spiritual growing pain that occurs in our relationship with God. Indeed, it occurs in any of our relationships that are maturing. Only if we allow our anxiety to refocus our attention on ourselves apart from God does the doubt become problematic.

Even Jesus had to struggle with this type of doubt as he grew in grace. In fact, his doubts confronted him in the guise of the trusted religious establishment. One day some Pharisees sidled up to Jesus and warned him confidentially to "leave this place and go somewhere else, for Herod the King wants to kill you." Having spoken recently with Moses and Elijah (Luke 9:28-36), Jesus already knew that another exodus was set to occur in Jerusalem. Now he had to decide if he really meant those wilderness words he had spoken about doing God's will and not his own. Should he ignore the advice of the Pharisees and enter Jerusalem and face certain execution? Or should he take their advice and avoid the great city and continue performing his acts of kindness? After all, his acts were pointing people to God.

Even though the words of warning spoken by the Pharisees were true, Jesus realized quickly that they were immaterial. Out in the wilderness, fighting against the forces of darkness trying to gain entry into his soul, Jesus had had to cling to his Father tenaciously even as he sought to do God's will. Hunger had weakened his body, and demonically-driven hallucinations had plagued his mind; but his resolve had remained firm. There in the wilderness he had discovered that God's will had little to do with realizing his own potential, and everything to do with glorifying God. He had refused to make his love of God conditional on God's expressed favor. Instead of demanding that God get him out of there, instead of becoming angry with God's Spirit for leading him in there, he had allowed his wilderness sojourn to teach him obedience. He had learned to entrust his life to God's character. "Your will be done in my life," he had said.

From that blessed moment forward, Jesus had known that he had a destiny from God to fulfill, a work of salvation to complete. He had also known that that work required that he enter the Holy City. Anything, then, that turned his head away from Jerusalem, even if it sounded as if it were in his own best interest, was a devilish temptation to distrust God. It didn't matter that the temptation came as a big-hearted gesture of concern from the religious leadership. God's will still had to be completed. Jesus' destiny awaited him in Jerusalem.

Trusting God as a sign of righteousness

We make a grievous error when we describe righteous people by what they do instead of by who they believe in. Righteousness before God is not a human act we perform. It is a divinely-promised identity we are offered, a divinely-given relationship we enjoy. It is a result of the covenant God offers us in Christ, a covenant modeled on the one made with Abraham.

Still puzzled by his earlier exchange with God, Abraham heard God say to him, "I am the LORD who brought you from Ur of the Chaldeans, to give you this land to possess." To which Abraham responded, "Yes, I know that, Lord. Actually, I was wondering if you still remembered! I am not as young as I used to be, you know! In fact, my body is as good as dead, if you catch my drift, Lord. How am I to know that these things truly are the certainties you keep telling me they are?" These were not strident words of insolence and irritation that Abraham spit out at God. They were a humble cry for God's help: "Lord, I do believe. Help me to overcome my unbelief!"

In response to Abraham's words, God did something absolutely remarkable. God signed a pact with a human being and said thereby, "I promise you!" When God made that first covenant of mercy with Abraham, God effectively said, "Abraham, you are right. It has been a while since I first made these promises, and you have been exceptionally patient with me. Beginning now, you may hold me accountable, too." God then told Abraham to prepare a sacrifice, and Abraham did so. Even then, he waited so long for God to come near that buzzards started settling upon his sacrifice. So, there was righteous, ninety-year-old Abraham tossing rocks and waving his staff and shooing off buzzards, undoubtedly muttering to himself the whole time, "God, I'm glad there's nobody here to see this!"

Finally, worn out from chasing buzzards all afternoon, Abraham fell into a deep sleep, and "a deep and terrifying darkness descended upon him." In the midst of that darkness, God not only accepted Abraham's sacrifice but actually confessed to him, "Abraham, this covenant isn't going to be easy for either you or me to keep. In fact, there will be times when you will lose this land for a while, but I promise it will still be yours. It will always be yours! And I will always be your God."

A covenant that promised us plenty of dirt and diapers would probably not strike most of us as a very religious sort of pact. In fact, depending on our state in life, it may not sound like much of a promise, period. After all, babies are something we choose to have! And if it is land we want, any old real estate agent can process the paperwork. But to a nomad like Abraham, divine promises of land and children were guarantees of tomorrow, not so unlike our own hopes for life eternal.

Our struggles for God today may not have us flailing away at buzzards. But if, in our estimation, God doesn't answer our prayers quickly enough, "a deep and terrifying darkness" is apt to settle upon us. But thanks be to God for this darkness! For even though it is spiritually disconcerting, under the cover of this darkness God does for us what we can't do for ourselves. God restores our hope! God accepts the sacrifice of obedience we offer and makes us wholly righteous in Jesus! By speaking a faithful word to us, God awakens our trust and establishes his covenant, confirming once again that God's name is still Emmanuel—"God with us." Come what may, God will *always* be with us.

God's covenant teaches us obedience

To be sure, the covenant that God makes with us is incredibly costly to God; for no matter how unfaithful Abraham's children have been, God has proven ever faithful to the promise he made first to Abraham. To this day, some four thousand years later, Abraham still has children and land. But land and kids are not all that God has promised. The covenant that God has established with each of us is just as sure, for it promises to supply all our needs in Christ Jesus. And it does; for Christ really is our only need in life, isn't he! We don't need meaningful worship or youth programs or nice homes or fulfilling jobs. Our only need is to see Christ and, having seen him, to be able to receive him.

Of course, keeping this covenant is a costly venture for us, too. As we walk the course Jesus has set for us, we discover continually that we still keep some areas of our lives back from God for ourselves, areas over which we are only now hearing Jesus say he wants to be Lord. These battles of faith are usually not petty skirmishes of a moral sort. More often, they are uncomfortable clashes with those deep-seated biases that we have never been willing to admit we have. They attack us at our emotional breaking points by exposing the instability of the false gods we have insisted on serving. They demand that we let go of the protective gear our world has supplied us. But lest we forget, these struggles of faith are not against a God who is seeking to wrest control away from us. They are the result of God's working within us and through us to empower us against the creeping cauldron of darkness that seeks to overtake us and ultimately to extinguish us.

Contrary to the entertainment-driven concerns of our culture, Scripture never once describes our faith walk as fun. Surprised? While there is an incredible joy in the journey, accepting and then keeping God's covenant is never described as easy. With "the man of God's own choosing" ("A Mighty Fortress Is Our God," Martin Luther) helping us along each step of the way, though, it is a good place to be. Indeed, it is the only right place to be. For we have a God who empowers us, a Christ who knows what we are going through, a community of faith that is praying for us and fighting alongside us. This is why we don't lose heart. We trust God in order to love God. We study with resolve to show ourselves approved. We invite God's people to offer us divine aid when we need it.

When the Pharisees offered Jesus a way to fulfill himself without having to deny himself, the offer was anything but rhetorical. Surely he knew that there would be many people who would forever ignore his sacrifice, and still others who would never even know that it had happened. Giving voice to our culture's inability to comprehend Jesus' acceptance of death and the humiliation the cross promised him, Brian Wren wrote poignantly,

> Here hangs a man discarded,
> a scarecrow hoisted high,
> a nonsense pointing nowhere
> to all who hurry by.
>
> Can such a clown of sorrows
> still bring a useful word
> where faith and love seem phantoms
> and every hope absurd?
>
> Yet here is help and comfort
> for lives by comfort bound,
> when drums of dazzling progress
> give strangely hollow sound.

("Here Hangs a Man Discarded," © 1975, 1995 by Hope Publishing Co., Carol Stream, IL 60188. All rights reserved. Used by permission.)

Today, we are offered the privilege of joining Christ in accepting God's will for our lives. Certainly we are thankful when this divine service suits our inclinations and builds us up. But we can trust God just as fully when God's service requires that we deny ourselves. Jesus had to accept the fact that it was not his place to try to control the events that swirled around him. Neither was it his place to make others understand why he chose a way that denied him rather than a way that could have fulfilled him. He had only to trust God that once the word was out, it would not return empty or void (Isaiah 55:11).

Conclusion

To address our doubt and keep us safe in those times when we are ready to give up our faith, God has made with us a covenant of grace. This word of creative, divine promise holds us firm when we grow weak. By trusting God to keep his word, by accepting this gift of covenant, we turn a corner in our own faith lives. For God's covenant is more than a simple word spoken. It is a redemptive word that includes four special gifts that make it possible for us to live faithfully. These gifts are community, reconciliation, memory, and humility. In each of the four remaining chapters, we will describe one of these gifts and discuss how our God uses it to build us up in grace.

Our work in this world is not nearly as important as the work of Christ. But its completion is just as necessary, for it is the work God has given us to do. The love we shower on guests, the good news of Jesus we share with strangers, the worship we extend to a God who loves us, the disciplines of fasting and giving of alms and praying—these are the mighty works God is calling each of us to accomplish in this world on behalf of the church. To this end we have been gifted by the Spirit of God. To this end we can be faithful and righteous, for God has promised!

Thanks be to God, who re-creates our spirits in love!

> We confess, O God, that we struggle against your covenant. Sometimes we consider your yoke of servanthood to be too tight and constrictive. At other times we prefer to choose our own course of action. At still other times we want to refocus your attention onto us rather than keeping our attention stayed on you. Too often our fears negate our trust and our doubts offset our hopes. Instead of learning your way, we have wanted to make your word conform to our way.
>
> Forgive us, we pray, for doubting your goodness and not praying for your will to be done with our lives. Conform our spirits to your great Spirit. Renew your covenant with us, and teach us to be a faithful people, that we may be resolute in our love and bring honor to your holy name. Lord, in your mercy, hear our prayer.

4 Community

Read: Isaiah 55:1-9; Psalm 63:1-8;
1 Corinthians 10:1-13; Luke 13:1-9

O God, who quenches our thirsty spirits by placing us in communities that love, stir up in us the desire to serve you together with our brothers and sisters.

Teach us to see you in the stranger, to feel you in the touch of a friend, to hear you in the call of the needy, to know you as you really are in Jesus Christ, your Son, our Lord, who lives and reigns with you and the Holy Spirit, one God, in glory ever-lasting. Amen.

It really is amazing how quickly Abraham's covenant children started griping about their treatment at God's hands. Less than three months removed from Egypt's bondage, the Israelites had become quite adept at blaming others whenever their journey took an unexpected turn. God was sustaining them daily with communal manna from heaven and with rocks that gave forth refreshing water when tapped with Moses' rod. But no matter how many times God offered assistance or came to the Israelites' rescue or showered them with divine love, they found something to gripe about. So it went for the next forty years. The people griped. The Lord responded with grace. The people wandered. The Lord led. The people wanted away. The Lord remained faithful.

It took a full forty years, but gradually, at times almost imperceptibly slowly, this people who didn't act like a people began to be re-formed and remolded into God's people. They certainly were not a loving people, at least not at first; but God kept showing them divine love. They certainly were not a faithful people, at least not at first; but God kept sharing with them divine faithfulness. It took a full generation, but eventually God's patience worked a divine miracle in these people, enabling them to reach a level of spiritual maturity that could, with some legitimacy, even be described as holy. Centuries later they were still appreciative that God had shown them mercy when all they had done was cry against God belligerently. "Let us sing to the LORD," they cried. "Let us make a joyful noise to the rock of our salvation!" (Psalm 95:1).

In our own day, anyone who attends church activities for any length of time will soon discover that God's people are still an imperfect people claiming to be one thing and appearing to be another. This is because Christians are imperfect people, which is not to say that they are hypocrites. Hypocrites are two-faced people who *pretend* to be what they are not. Christians are disciples, a people who are *learning* to be what they are not. This is an important distinction that can counter the rampant cynicism of our age. It is a helpful reminder that our righteousness is never the result of our actions but is instead the source of our new identities.

In all likelihood, it will take us a whole lifetime of loving God and serving our neighbor before our claims and our actions will begin to resemble each other very fully. And yet, thanks be to God, our grace-laden baptisms have started us on these journeys. We may sometimes feel as if we are a band of struggling pilgrims who are wandering around in meaningless circles like the ancient Israelites once did, but we are pilgrims all the same. As we mature and leave our idols behind us, though, we will discover that our desert wanderings have been leading us all along to the edge of the Promised Land. We may be an imperfect people, but we are still the church because God says we are, still called to be holy because God wants us to be holy, still called to praise God because that is our one purpose in life.

But how are we to live with this tension of realizing that God has called us to press on to perfection every moment of every day, all the time knowing that our actions leave so much to be desired? It is enough to make us wonder how the authors of Scripture could refer to imperfect disciples like us as saints!

God's covenant creates a new people

Thankfully, we are not the first who have had to come to terms with this dilemma. Like many of the churches mentioned in the New Testament, the church in Corinth is one that ought to give us hope. Corinth is a wonderful example of what the church is often like—not what it should be like, but what it is like. Hardly a model church, it was divided internally and antagonistic toward outsiders, with all sorts of caucus groups vying for control. To be sure, it was full of devout people who prayed regularly and sought the face of God. But it was also full of not-so-devout people who did little to deepen their walk of faith. It was full of people who strived to serve God with every fiber of their being. It was also full of people who tried to get away with everything they could.

In light of this church's mixed character, it is intriguing that Paul called this church a holy church, full of sanctified people whom God loved. "You are not lacking in any spiritual gift," he told them. And he was right. Everything necessary to have a faithful, holy church existed in that community, just as it does in our churches today with the people presently attending them. To be sure, no one person has the ability to perform all the faithful work of the church, for the church, in any church. That is a work God has given to the *whole* church to do *as* the church, a work we accomplish by working together in reliance upon the One who first gave us these gifts. It is a work that, instead of puffing us up, always brings glory to God, always builds up Christ, always shares the light of Jesus with the nations.

Through the covenant established with us in Jesus, God routinely makes us into a community people. This is not an easy thing to accomplish, though; for we all come to God initially as the individuals our culture tells us we are. At first, not one of us is particularly adept at praising God or praying to God or studying about God or communing with God. Neither are we particularly concerned about those who live near us or those who wait on us or those who work with us. We are not even very concerned about the people who worship with us. But no matter how awe-inspiring our individual credentials may be, they mean nothing apart from the community of faith that accepts us in the name of Jesus. This is where we learn that our personal destinies are really communal gifts, offerings from God mediated through God's holy people. God never asks God's people to perform superhuman feats or even to rise up and make the church great. To the contrary, we are invited to glorify God; but since the worship of God is always a communal act, we will need one another's help to accomplish that.

Communities of faith teach us to mature spiritually

When we accept the covenant of grace that we are offered in Jesus, we embark on a divine experiment that promises to lead us ultimately into the eternally worshipful presence of God. But what about in the meantime? How does God sanctify our souls and make our hearts righteous like Abraham?

The first of many gifts we are offered by the Spirit to complete this work of sanctification is a community of like-minded, perfect-hearted people who love God and worship Jesus and depend upon the Spirit. Just as we are physically born into families we didn't choose, so we are spiritually reborn and placed by God in faith communities we didn't choose. Selected by God to be our faith mentors, these communities provide us the resources necessary for us to mature spiritually into God's likeness. They model for us humility. They pass on to us their love of God's Word. They show us how to be generous. By their example they teach us how to be Christians. Our spiritual apprenticeship to them is a form of God's great love; for contrary to what our culture tells us, we do not choose our own destinies. We are formed by those who precede us, instructed by those who tell us "the glorious deeds of the LORD" (Psalm 78:4).

Contrary to another of our cultural biases, though, the community of faith that we are a part of is not limited to those people we see on Sundays. It also includes the creedal witness of the church across the centuries. It is present in the hammered-out liturgies of Word and Table we use weekly. It speaks through the canon of Scripture written by prophets and apostles, adopted by bishops, read daily by God's faithful. It lifts its melodic voice in constant praise to God via hymns prayed and sung devotionally. It offers its example of holy love through saintly acts of sacrifice remembered and through martyr words of witness spoken. It exists wherever and whenever faithful saints of God have joined their hearts and loved one another.

Whether through books they have written, prayers they have offered, or examples of faith they continue to live, the community of God's people teaches us that every act we perform and every word we speak can be so holy that it glorifies God. No wonder it takes a lifetime for faith to be crafted within us!

No matter how much like Christ we become, we continue to need a faith community to sustain and deepen our faith. Indeed, one of the spiritual truths we quickly discover in our walk with Jesus is how regularly we need the insights, critiques, and encouragement of our fellow travelers in grace. Sometimes this is because we face strange or new situations, and we need to rely on others more experienced than we are to give us hope or to guide us through our plight. At other times it is because we are unable to think clearly about the predicaments we find ourselves in, and we need others to offer us their fresh or different perspectives. At still other times it is because we are prone to sweep difficult issues under the rug, and we need others to hold us accountable and to force us to do the right thing.

Communities of faith hold us accountable

Several years ago I made a poor business decision that affected the best friend I had in seminary. At one level it wasn't really a big deal. I mean, nobody lost anything. I had agreed to share with my friend some free books that we had obtained from a publisher, but I ended up giving them to another student who was pressuring me for them. The act certainly wasn't premeditated on my part, but it did involve a breach of promise. Once it happened, it was easier simply to pretend it hadn't happened than to deal with it honestly. My friend, however, would not let the issue slide; and in the process he taught me an important lesson about the value of and the risks involved in a true friendship. One afternoon, with nobody else around, he let me know that he didn't appreciate what I had done (see Matthew 18:15). My first thought was, "You just need to get over it! You have no right to be angry with me about that!" But I didn't say anything. After I had had some time to think about it, I realized he was right. And I had to try to make amends for it.

Have you ever confronted someone you really loved? Have you ever held him or her accountable when he or she didn't want to be held that way? If you have, you know something about the value and importance of communities of faith. Jesus said that friends are willing to lay down their lives for one another (John 15:13). Sometimes in communities of faith we have to place a friendship at risk in order to restrain the friend from endangering himself or herself or from placing the community in jeopardy. My friend trusted me enough to hope that I would respond appropriately to his words of rebuke. By trusting me that much, he showed me that he had more faith in me than I had in him; for I'm not sure that I would have confronted him had the tables been turned.

If you have ever found yourself in a similar situation before God, you know that in moments like these there is nowhere to hide. There is nowhere to run. Life is reduced to a confession of guilt, and God does for us the one thing we so intensely fear might happen: God shows us the mercy we need. That mercy makes us feel terribly uncomfortable; for contrary to our world, which treats us like immature kids incapable of bearing responsibility for our identity—or lack thereof, God expects us to grow up. God's mercy shared with me through my friend was not a friendly pat on the back accompanied by the message that I was really okay, just victimized by others or misunderstood by him. Through my friend's words, God's mercy confronted my evil and demanded its removal. Most importantly, it offered me the means necessary to accomplish that removal. It offered me a community that cared about me.

When talking with his spiritually young children in Corinth, Paul often found himself discussing topics that didn't sound terribly important at first, like the eating of foods that had been prepared for pagan sacrifices. To the young in faith or the impatient in Spirit, the importance of these conversations for faith development is often missed. In reality, communal mentors regularly use such conversations to confront our evil and offer us God. In Corinth, for instance, some of the church members carefully avoided purchasing meats that were being sold in the temple marketplaces. Other members had no qualms about either buying or eating the meat. "Meat's meat," they said. "And idols aren't really real. Why, then, all these prohibitions by the church? Why worry about the personal history of a slice of meat?"

The argument made sense. Paul admitted as much. He couldn't have cared less where a particular piece of meat had come from. But he also realized that the core issue being raised by the church in Corinth was not about eating food that had been sacrificed to idols. It wasn't even about what goes in or what comes out of a person's mouth (Matthew 15:11). The issue was Christian maturity and its implications for how we live our day-to-day lives. Are we trying to serve God *while* we retain our old habits and vices? Or is our service to God changing the way we live, the things we do, the choices we make, the words we speak, the people we see? When personal choices clash with communal purposes, which is more important? Our culture has no doubt on this score. Thankfully, those who seek to ground their beliefs in Scripture and their actions in the traditions of a faith community that stretches across two millennia know otherwise. *There is neither scriptural nor traditional warrant for an attitude that elevates the individual at the expense of the community.* The Christians at Corinth thought that all they had to do to love God was to fit God into their belief systems. Paul had the task of teaching them that their belief systems needed to conform to the Christian community's understanding of God.

Communities of faith restrain our sin

In Corinth, church members were testing God by testing the spiritual boundaries established by God. They were seeing how involved they could be *with* idolatry without actually being involved *in* idolatry. They wanted to see how far they could push God, how thinly they could stretch God's grace and still legitimately call themselves Christian. Paul said that this kind of testing of the Lord was really a temptation to ignore the words of God. Given license, it would tear the church apart into a loose confederation of competing truth claims. We continue this line of unholy reasoning today whenever we try to see how far we can separate ourselves from the church and still remain a part of the church, or when we try to figure out how little we can do at church or give to the church and remain accepted by God.

We have been placed by God in communities of grace so that our faith can become filled with superlatives, not diminutives. The question is not, How *little* can we get away with giving or doing? but, How *much* can we give! How *much* can we do! Jesus has no interest in competing with other gods by offering us gifts that titillate. He insists that we enter fully into a community of faith so that he can offer us the one gift that truly matters—himself!

FINDING CHRIST, FINDING LIFE

The Corinthian Christians wanted the unqualified freedom to act without any restraints being imposed upon them by the wishes or needs of others. They wanted to eat meats that had previously been sacrificed to idols, regardless of what some people thought about that. But that kind of self-centered, unrestrained lifestyle is not the way the Christian life teaches. We are called to give ourselves away in the promotion of righteousness and Christian freedom. Our way of life should always promote Christian behavior and draw people to God and increase our love to our fellow human beings.

For Paul, it is not the weak and the faithless who are in the greatest danger of falling spiritually. It is those who think they are standing firm by themselves, those who are trying to live independently of the body of Christ, those who think that everything in life is okay just as it is. But it is not those people who appear tough as nails who are most okay. It is those who discover that the only way to emerge victorious in life is by becoming vulnerably open to one another. You see, we really have nothing in life to cause us to boast. Our achievements are always the achievements of Christ at work in us. Our good deeds are always a result of the presence of the Holy Spirit in our lives.

Even the temptations we experience are not exceptional, says Paul. They are just the same old tired temptations that are common to people everywhere, in every time. They are, for instance, the way our discontent with God shows itself most visibly; for they encourage us to deny God and to focus our attention on ourselves. Idolatry tempts us to assert our own wills and to set our own rules for life. Sexual immorality tempts us to let our passions rule without any thought of responsibility toward or compassion for others. Testing the Lord tempts us to be cynical and faithless as we inevitably do as we please. Grumbling tempts us to express with growing brazenness our dissatisfaction toward the ways of God.

With such a formidable group of community-destroying temptations presenting themselves to us at every turn, it is a matter of amazing grace that we ever emerge victorious over them. Paul was right, though. Our personal temptations are really communal temptations, common to everyone. We don't have it any tougher than the next person. God is ever faithful to us and will not allow us to be tempted beyond what we can bear at any moment in life. When temptation draws near, God draws nearer still and provides us a way out so that we can stand up under the temptation.

Communities of faith teach us to overcome common temptation not by exerting our will but by fixing our minds on the pioneer and perfecter of our faith, the human God named Jesus, who helps us stand fast. We overcome temptation because God desires us to, because God provides us the means of doing so, because we are seeking to glorify God in everything we do. We overcome temptation by asking God to manifest the grace of God in our lives by helping us get beyond ourselves and begin living our lives for others. There is just no other way but to trust God and obey!

Conclusion

Clinging to God, choosing the life of God over the death that denies God, is something we learn to do in community. It is something we do as community, with one another, if we intend to do it at all. And having to rely on one another is scary. In fact, it is openly disturbing, because I don't want to be your keeper any more than I want you to be mine. I suspect that you feel the same way. I have no interest in my eternal destiny with God being contingent on your desire or lack of desire for God, for that forces me to realize that I am not the one who controls this thing. My salvation is in the hands of God, who is calling others as faithfully as he is calling me. I would prefer to believe that it is possible for me to have a torrid love affair with God all by myself without having to have anything to do with anyone else. But that is not the way God has designed this relationship of grace we have been given. Those are not the terms of the covenant we have been offered. If I am to accept fully the covenant of God and choose life instead of death, I can't even pretend to be able to cling to God all by myself. *I come to God holding your hand, or I don't come at all.* In the same way, *you come to God holding my hand, or you don't come at all.*

When the scales finally fall from our eyes and the calluses wear off our hearts, the community of faith will have done its job with us. It will have taught us to see Jesus as he truly is by accepting him where he may be found. In words that we know only God can speak, we will then hear him say to us, "*I am* the one you have been seeking all along. I have found you. I have called you. I love you." Such is the power of God's transforming love, offered to us in the communities of faith we worship in weekly.

Thanks be to God!

We confess, O God, that we have tried to live a life of faith on our own, in our own way. When we fail to understand the church's teachings, we assume its teachings are out of date. When we fail to hear your call, we assume you are nowhere to be found. When we become upset with the people we worship with, we usually choose to leave in a huff rather than to seek the reconciliation you have told us to pursue.

Forgive us, we pray, for our faulty thinking and our faulty living. Grant us the mercy to live with one another on earth in imitation of the way you live in community in heaven. Break down the barriers that still separate us, that we may love as you have first loved us. Lord, in your mercy, hear our prayer.

5 Reconciliation

Read: Joshua 5:9-12; Psalm 32;
2 Corinthians 5:16-21; Luke 15:1-3, 11b-32

O God, who feeds your people and makes them one, heal the divisions that not only splinter your church but also starve your children.

Create in us clean hearts that thrive on peace, that we might work to restore unity in your Body, even as we share with others the love of Jesus Christ, your Son, our Lord, who lives and reigns with you and the Holy Spirit, one God, in glory ever-lasting. Amen.

When we first accept the covenant of grace God offers us, our lives begin to change. Re-created in God's likeness, we are re-formed into Christ's image, empowered by the Spirit's gifts. The Spirit calls us to and places us in communities that hold us responsible and teach us to be faithful. Filled with peace and destined for glory, we can think of nothing we would rather do than spend our time in the presence of God, worshiping God, loving God's people.

In this state of spiritual bliss, we are tempted to think that our worries about sin are a thing of our past. This mistake is common and has plagued the church since its inception. To be sure, we who believe in Jesus are spiritually reborn and adopted into God's one family. Made the humble bearers of new hearts, our identities have been changed forever. But we must be careful here. The power of the old ways that once filled us with the illusion of contentment has been broken, but these ways have not yet been destroyed. These old ways can still lure us away from God with their flashy appeals of quick success and easy acceptance and bodily happiness. If we are honest, we know there are times when we fall prey to the old ways' advances. Lured away by their enticing promises of a more satisfying life, we turn our backs on the covenant of God. We turn our backs on the community of faith.

Despite the fact that God has given us mentors that teach us and church families that support us, despite the fact that God has established with us a covenant of grace that offers us new life, there are still times when we rebel openly against God. We close our ears to the voice of the Spirit. We thumb our noses at Christ. Deciding that we know better than

God how to live our lives, we take matters into our own hands and try to do again as we once pleased.

This state of rebellion is what the church calls "sin in believers." Deep within each of us are unholy biases, unchristian thoughts, impure ways of speech, unfaithful habits that have yet to be rooted out of us. Although Christ is faithful to bring these matters to our attention and to cleanse us of all unrighteousness (1 John 1:9), we sometimes decide to engage in, rather than to dispense with, the sin in question. If we are not careful, these solitary acts of rebellion can quickly become ingrained patterns of sin again. Call it a lack of perseverance, a loss of courage, an inattentiveness to the Spirit, the point is that we turn our backs on God. Like the prodigal younger son who impatiently demanded his inheritance from his father, we walk away, or at least do our best to walk away. For a time we may even succeed.

But once we have known the joy of salvation, life apart from God is just not what it is chalked up to be. Indeed, out on our own again we learn an important lesson of faith that surprises us even as it frustrates us. We discover that the old ways no longer satisfy us. To our amazement, however, we also discover that the church's talk of covenant and community is not just spiritual rhetoric. Despite our wandering, God remains true to the covenant. In Christ, God declares that we have become new people. As Paul said, the old has gone! The new has come!

To be sure, there is never any excuse for our sin; but thanks be to God, *there is always justification for it*. No matter where we wander, we cannot go so far that we are beyond the love of God (Psalm 139:7-12). No matter what we do, we can always come home to Christ. No matter how pervasive the sin, we can hear the Spirit's call on our lives.

Would to God that once we accepted God's offer of grace, we would not have to worry about sin in our lives. But we do. This side of the grave, believers must continue to struggle against the unholy reality of sin. Not only must we struggle against it but we must learn what to do on those occasions when we commit sin ourselves. That is why, along with the covenant God has made with us and the community God has placed us in, God also offers us a second gift, the gift of reconciliation.

The prodigal younger son

Speaking to the Pharisees and scribes at the end of his life, Jesus told a parable about a prodigal son, a parable that has become something of a cult favorite for many people. The story is full of intense drama, believable characters, surprising plots. A young man decides that he no longer wishes to live under his father's jurisdiction. He demands his inheritance and leaves home. For a time he enjoys being out from under his father's rule. But once the inheritance is spent and his friends have fled, he is reduced to performing demeaning jobs just to stay alive. Only then does he remember home with a bit of fondness. Eventually tiring of his so-called freedom, he decides to go home and take his chances with his father.

The boy's decision to go home is what the church calls reconciliation. When we reconcile, we "make peace with." Reconciliation is an important and vital part of our Christian experience. This is why our pastors allow us time to share the peace of Christ with one another in our worship. Because there are times when we falter, this time of sharing the peace provides us the opportunity to make things right with one another. More than a time to say hello to people, we use this time to make peace with those we have abandoned or to share peace with those who have hurt us.

One of the most common ways we have of talking about reconciliation with God is in terms of being found. This language is true both to Scripture and to our hymnody. Twice in Jesus' story to the Pharisees, he had the father say, "My son was lost and has been found." John Newton's "Amazing Grace" personalized the message by casting us as the younger sibling, enabling us to say, "*I* once was lost, but now am found."

I want to suggest, however, that Jesus' story does an even better job of describing our salvation in terms of coming home. That is important, for these days I find few Christians struggling with feelings of being "lost" theologically. No, they are struggling with the rampant individualism of our culture. Each of us knows what it feels like to be in the company of strangers, away from home, separated from those who love us. Secretly we long for the courage to drop the smiles that mask our shame or hurt or fear. We just want to be ourselves again. We want to be real, without the pretense.

Another struggle we Christians face daily is the desire to enjoy more fully the good life as it has been defined by the world around us. But the way our culture teaches us to do this requires that we turn our backs on God, who has taught us differently. This tension places us in a quandary, for Jesus has told us that we cannot serve both God and money (Matthew 6:24). Neither can we be great without choosing to be least, or first without being last (Matthew 20:16, 26). In speaking like this, Jesus is not offering alternatively acceptable ways for Christians to make money or achieve lasting fame. He is reminding all who long for the kingdom of God that fame is fleeting, that "the love of money is a root of all kinds of evil" (1 Timothy 6:10).

Like the younger brother in Jesus' story, there are times when we too make poor choices. We learn to demand our inheritance early, to mortgage our futures, to spend our tomorrows. Refusing to worry about the adverse effect on our souls, we leave behind everything that defines us, including our family, including our community of faith. Were it not for the faithful voice of God's parental Spirit, we might forever forget the homes we have abandoned.

To be sure, spending our inheritance free of the oversight of our father can be fun, but only for a time. For in time our fascination with nights out begins to wear thin; the exhausting nature of our enslaving jobs begins to wear heavy. Even the homes we have built and the toys we have purchased cease to hold our fancy. We are fenced off from our neighbors, and life grows empty. The more separate we become from one another, the deeper grows our sense of alienation from one another. One of the most troubling signs of this even more troubling truth is the fact that we no longer care even to sit together in restaurants; we prefer to "drive through," to eat imprisoned in the freedom of the solitary confinement offered by our cars as we dash madly from one engagement to the next. The whole thing is as ludicrous as sitting in a pigsty sucking on carob pods, fantasizing about the good life we're enjoying now that we are free of our father's oversight!

According to Jesus, there is only one way out of this devilishly ingenious prison we've self-constructed. Like the son in the parable, we need to come to ourselves. We may have grown tired of home and family and the missional chores our dad expected us to complete, but we need to come home. No matter how fully we have abandoned our Christ-centered identities and left for parts unknown to do as we please, when the Spirit calls us home, we need to go. For the Spirit is inviting us to remember who we are, whose child we have become, whose name we bear! The Spirit is sharing with us the divine truth that no matter what we do in life, we cannot sever the familial ties that bind us to our mother or to our father. Sure, we can deny them for a time, but we cannot sever them. We may be emotionally spent. We may be spiritually exhausted. But in response to the father's bidding, we need to come home. Indeed, it is a word of gospel that we *can* come home!

Many of us have. Remembering something back home that sustained us once upon a time, and wondering if it might still be available in some limited quantity, we turned our hearts toward home, hoping it wasn't too late. Knowing we had squandered our relationship with our Father, knowing we had made unreasonable demands before running away, we certainly did not come home expecting a banquet to be thrown in our honor. We just wanted to live and to experience love again. And so, by the grace of God, we have. Much to our surprise, though, God has immediately shared with us a meal and embraced us in love. And in these moments of divine forgiveness and loving reconciliation, "the love that made us makes us one" (From "I Come With Joy," by Brian Wren. Words © 1971 Hope Publishing Co. Used by permission.). We may have left and become strangers for a time, but we have become friends again.

The meal of reconciliation

As a rule, meals have never meant that much to me. Because I have never had to worry where my next meal would come from, I have usually taken meals for granted. Except by personal choice, I have never gone hungry. You probably haven't, either.

Because I have lived amid so much food, I have had trouble grasping the significant, albeit ambiguous, role that food plays in Scripture. Sometimes it is used to cover heinous crimes, as when Eve talked with a snake while eating some fruit, or when Cain killed Abel over food he had offered God. At other times it provides a context for experiencing forgiving love, as when Joseph revealed himself to his brothers at a banquet, or when Jesus broke bread and ate fish after his resurrection, in the presence of disciples who did not recognize him. The point is, many of the biblical stories occur around tables, at mealtime, in the presence of food. So, incidentally, does our worship!

Twelve years ago my wife and I wandered into a United Methodist church down the street from where we lived. Up to that point in time, I had never even considered attending The United Methodist Church. The only United Methodist preacher I had ever heard speak was at my sister's baccalaureate. He was a strange-looking guy, dressed in what looked like a white bathrobe. His sermon consisted of waving a can of salt in the air, now and again pouring out little mounds of salt onto the school stage, and urging all the graduating seniors to be the salt of the earth. I thought to myself, *no wonder The United Methodist Church is losing so many members!*

But we were desperately hungry for some spiritual nourishment and actively looking for a new church home. Tired of eating the leftover pods we were being fed, we were willing to try anything, even a United Methodist church. Besides, it was the closest church to where we lived; so we went. There, for the first time in my life, I discovered through the church's liturgy not only how famished I actually was but also how I, too, had been demanding my inheritance and spending my future apart from God. And when the invitation to the Table was given to all who were baptized, even though I decided to watch rather than to participate in the meal since my wife had not yet been baptized, I discovered the holy importance of gathering in living faith around the one Table of God.

There I watched little children hold hands and dance and skip their way toward the Table, wearing big smiles on their faces. I watched as old men hobbled on canes and women held on to each other's arms. Still others depended on walkers as they made their way slowly but with great purpose and resolve toward that same Table. I watched young men and women in the prime of their lives bow in humility at that Table. I watched as a diverse congregation was melded into one body, not by the sermon that had been preached, but by a common meal of bread and wine that was being eaten.

I had always taken that meal for granted, but no more. As I wiped tears from my eyes, I knew in that moment that not only did I want to be United Methodist, but I wanted desperately to share in the intimate holiness of that sacred meal. For as I watched the procession that morning as a kind of spectator, I felt the most overwhelming sense of loneliness and emptiness I have ever experienced in my life. I didn't even know those people who were congregating around that Table, and yet somehow I knew that they were my long-lost family. I longed to be one with them in a way I had never even dreamed was possible before. I wanted to be embraced and loved by them. I wanted to hold out my hands to Jesus, just as they had, and to receive in return the blessed body of Christ. That's the kind of holy union that occurs around banquet tables at which Christ is present. That is the holy gift of reconciliation that God shares with his children over supper.

The prodigal elder son

But there is more to Jesus' story than a single child gone amuck. There is a second son in the story, a prodigal elder son who is just as unappreciative of his home as was his younger sibling. He may have stayed home the whole time, but he too despised his father's character. In the end, he was as prodigal as the younger son.

The elder religious brothers, the scribes and Pharisees, were growing increasingly upset with Jesus for good reason. They understood quite well the implications not only of Jesus' actions at table but also of this story he told. Quite frankly, they didn't want to be made one with the snotty-nosed kids and the hobbled old folk whom Christ was uniting and loving and granting new dignity. They thought they were too good for that.

One of the sad things about the church today is that there are as many prodigal elder children sitting in the pews as there are prodigal younger children who have left. Though their sin has not led them to leave home like their younger siblings, it is as great. The trouble is, they have yet to realize that they too are prodigal. Nevertheless, the joy of their close relationship to God is just as shriveled up in them as it is in their younger brothers and sisters. They too are sinful. They go through the motions of the work God gives them—serving on committees, teaching Sunday school—thinking that these acts should satisfy God, not realizing that God has given them their work as a sign of love to share with others and to help others mature in their faith. Indeed, they have taken God's grace for granted for so long that they don't even recognize how hard their hearts have grown. Present in body but not in spirit, they are frustrated and miserable in their own Father's house, unwilling to let go of the pent-up passion that increasingly defines them.

The sin of the elder sibling is not the active committing of morally culpable deeds that separate us from God. It is the kind of passive neglect that accompanies our refusal to love. It is the substitution of spiritual busyness for the formation of godly character. We begin to take for granted our relationship with our Father. Acting as if our work should endear us to God, we are not the least bit thrilled to discover that our Father loves our prodigal younger brothers and sisters every bit as much as he does us. Having worked in the church like common slaves, we think Dad ought to appreciate our sacrifice and reward us accordingly, not pander to our faithless siblings when they dare to come home.

That is not going to happen, though; for our God is not our foreman. God is our Father. And our relationship to our Father is not based on the amount of work we accomplish; it is grounded in the undying love the Father has for us. We are not our dad's nameless servants! We never have been! We are our God's friends (John 15:15)! We could have been living this whole time as the blessed sons and daughters we are. But to do so now, we will have to let go of our pent-up anger and agree to become part of the family again.

In the parable Jesus told, the father went out to meet the younger son. He invited the son to come in to share the feast. Interestingly, he went out to meet the elder son too, pleading with him to come in and enjoy the festivities. Unwilling that either of his spiritually prodigal children should perish, the father kept a vigilant watch out for the first signs of a repentant spirit. When those signs appeared in his younger son, he welcomed his child home to share with him liberally from the inexhaustible riches of his household. To this day our God is glorified when the estranged community gathers around a common Table to dine at a banquet feast. Indeed, God too is reconciled there!

The younger son accepted his father's offer and came in, and we are left in little doubt that his destiny was secure in the father's love. The unrepentant anger of the elder son, however, leaves us wondering if he ever chose to come in or not. Like the Pharisees and scribes of old, some of us are being invited to come in and eat the feast. The food is plentiful, but we are having none of it. The peace still passes all understanding, but we are refusing to receive it.

Conclusion

Every week we assemble as a prodigal people who need to be reconciled, both to God and to one another. Whether we are elder brothers or younger sisters, we come together to hear God's offer of grace renewed. We gather around a table to receive the meal that accompanies that offer. The trouble is, we have some difficulty believing that there is anything holy that happens around tables, even those Tables at which Christ is present.

All the same, just as the father offered the fatted calf to the younger son, just as he reminded the elder son that the riches of the household were available to him all along, so God through this meal restores our dignity, makes us righteous, and reminds us of our hope in Christ. The reconciliation that God offers us in Jesus is much more than a gift. It is a ministry of participation. We are made God's righteousness in order that we might share that righteousness with those around us.

To be sure, God shares with us the peace of reconciliation in a variety of ways and places. While it is not dispensed to us solely at the Table, this is the place it occurs preeminently. Only after *dining* with his disciples did Jesus say to them, "Peace I leave with you; my peace I give to you" (John 14:27).

These days, of course, it is no longer a fatted calf that is served at the common Table. It is a slain lamb! It is our *other* brother, if you will—the brother who, out of his own prodigal love for us siblings, freely gave away his life. Trusting in God alone, he believed that his sacrificial act would one day reunite our estranged family and "make us one with Christ, one with each other, and one in ministry to all the world" ("A Service of Word and Table I," *The United Methodist Hymnal;* © 1972, 1980, 1985, 1989 The United Methodist Publishing House; Used by permission; page 10).

Would to God that we might experience this reconciliation ourselves, even a people like us! May Christ come quickly, and give us his peace!

We confess, O God, that we are your prodigal children. We have been led astray by the world's promises of happiness and contentment. We may still be in the church, but there is no joy in our lives. Our families are divided. Our spirits are famished. Our hearts are cold. Coming home seems like a childish figment of our imagination. Letting go of our self-righteous anger seems more than we can bear. What are we to do?

Forgive us, we pray, for shying away from your Table. We are as afraid to believe in your gift of reconciliation as we are to accept it. Continue to be more prodigal with your love than we are toward your grace. Offer us your peace. Heal our troubled spirits. Make your family whole again. Lord, in your mercy, hear our prayer.

6 Memory

Read: Isaiah 43:16-21; Psalm 126;
          Philippians 3:4b-14; John 12:1-8

O God, who renews our minds and transforms our spirits, shake us loose from the lethargy that steals our joy and evades your sanctifying grace.

Inspire us to sing your praises and worship your glory, that we may remember with gladness the mighty acts you have accomplished in us through Jesus Christ, your Son, our Lord, who lives and reigns with you and the Holy Spirit, one God, in glory everlasting. Amen.

These days we do not have to go far to find people who, despairing of any change for the better, have given up expecting life to be very satisfying. They are simply going through the motions of living, enduring the trauma of one bad relationship after another, afraid to ask for help, too embarrassed to receive help. Financially they are chasing after an economic happiness that is unreachable. Spiritually they are listening to any New Age rhetoric that promises relief to their troubled souls. Even people who have remained within the church are apt to feel stymied, helpless, out of control. They are as unsure how to address the symptoms that appear in their own lives as they are unclear how to heal the woes of those around them. To compensate, they try to exploit the moment for all it is worth, for the moment is about all any of us seem to have anymore. Increasingly unaware of what they are to do with God's mercy, they live with little meaning in life and even less hope for life.

Frustrated and full of fear, people will do almost anything to try to achieve some personal control over the events of tomorrow. It is a situation tailor-made for shysters to ply their trade. Because we all long for some prophet to rise up and speak some sense into our senselessness, all that anybody needs to do to obtain a hearing these days is wax clairvoyant and claim to be able to discern the future. However, contrary to what is popularly believed, tomorrow is not predetermined, and prophecy has little to do with decoding the future ahead of time so that we can prepare for it more adequately today.

Oh, I know there are people who will swear by the extended five-day weather forecasts that appear in the paper. There are others who will stake their financial futures on stock market trends and their various indicators. And heaven knows it can be fun to break open a fortune cookie at the restaurant or to laugh at the ridiculous comments made in a horoscope table. But we take the "prophetic voices" in our world that predict the outcome of life tomorrow much too seriously when we try to maneuver ourselves into a position to take advantage of the advice they offer.

Unfortunately, church people are not free of this problem, especially when we engage in the construction of charts that purport to map out the order of the end times. To be sure, the consummation of human history and the final judgment of Jesus are vital doctrines of the church and of paramount importance to us. However, despite all the claims to the contrary, scriptural prophecy is not about who gets raptured when, or how the millennium will be ushered in. This popular understanding of prophecy has become a lucrative market that false prophets have invaded in order to fleece God's sheep and line their own pockets!

The prophetic call of God on our lives does not invite us to analyze what *tomorrow* may be like. Instead, it reminds us to remember *yesterday*. It summons us to remain true to the Spirit's call, for prophecy is not a prediction made about events yet to be. It is a proclamation shared about who we are today, a declaration made about the faithful character of our covenant God. It is a history lesson that teaches us to remember how God has acted before.

In other words, prophecy is always a summons to entrust our lives to the care of God. It is an invitation to allow the Spirit to re-form our lives into the image of Jesus. Above all, it is a call to worship, for it is preeminently in the act of praising God that we remember all that God has done. In remembering God's mighty acts accomplished on our behalf, we are made a resilient people, strong enough to overcome the fears we face daily.

Remembering God's mighty acts is an act of faithful living

As we strive daily to live faithfully, we learn in hope to fix our eyes fully upon Jesus. Contrary to the deep and growing sense of resignation that pervades our culture, our worship of God grounds our Spirit-invested lives in the hope of Jesus' salvation. Despite the rhetoric we hear regularly, the goal of history has little to do with the formation of utopian societies or the management of financially lucrative empires. Indeed, the goal of history is not even a thing we manage. It is a Person we are set free to love. The goal of history has been enfleshed already in the God-man named Jesus. We may see all this through a glass darkly right now, but by looking steadfastly upon Jesus, we can begin to see what God wills for us all to be like.

That is precisely the type of advice that the prophet Isaiah was offering to Israel at a time when Israel's culture was collapsing about her. Try as they could to put a good face on the collapse, political leaders in Israel knew that it was only a matter of time until Israel's demise. Mighty Assyria in the north was on the march, relentlessly gobbling up petty fiefdoms with reckless abandon. Hope for any kind of good life tomorrow was all but gone. But instead of glossing over the political realities of his day or pretending the situation was not as bleak as it appeared, Isaiah confronted the great darkness gathering on Israel's borders by speaking an even mightier word of divine hope. He called on the people to renew their flagging spirits.

In itself, Isaiah's message is not all that surprising. After all, we have all heard preachers give us sermonic pep talks designed to brighten our flagging spirits. What makes Isaiah's words seem so strange to us is that he refused to encourage Israel to trust its good feelings or to dwell in its mountaintop experiences. Instead, he offered the people new hope for tomorrow by reminding them of God's faithful actions yesterday. Recalling the remarkable events of the Exodus, he spoke of God's actions of almost a thousand years before, claiming that they were a present reality still. The Lord "makes a way in the sea," he reminded the people, "a path in the mighty waters." God rescues us from all those who try to harm us.

What Isaiah understood was something we have all but forgotten. Our trust is to be in God, not in our own faith! When life is in great flux, we have an even greater need to worship God, to know that there are some spiritual constants that hold true in life. We need to know that our God "is the same yesterday and today and forever" (Hebrews 13:8). Isaiah did for his time what all the true Israelite prophets from Moses on had done in their times. He refused to make predictions about the future based on his personal assessments of the leadership potential or political might or economic strength of Israel. Instead, he called the people to worship God. He called Israel to reflect on the terms of the covenant that God had made with them (compare Deuteronomy 4:25-31). He knew that it is never our political savvy that carries the day, nor our brute strength that relieves our pesky fears. The only thing that matters is our adherence to the faith-filled covenant of God.

But, trained skeptics that we are, we immediately want to know how we can be so sure of this. It is one thing to say that God is faithful and keeps his word, but how do we really know that God can be trusted? The only way we can prove God's faithfulness to the covenant is by taking the risk of entrusting our lives to God's care. God invites us to become familiar with the terms of the covenant so that we can understand the whole of our history in light of those terms. That is what all the great prophets of Israel called the people to do, time and again. In times of great crisis, the people assembled—they re-membered—to rehearse the mighty acts of God. Together they recalled not only the many ways God had rescued them from their enemies but also the many times God had held them accountable to the covenant they had accepted.

Remembering the past is not an invitation to dwell in the past

Remembering the past does not mean that God desires us to seek asylum from tomorrow by escaping into the confines of yesterday. We remember faithfully only when we meditate upon the God who came to us *yesterday*, who remains present with us *today*, who promises to be worthy of our trust *tomorrow*. In other words, we are to develop faithful memories of God so that we can resist two urges: first, to reinhabit our own sinful pasts; and second, to be so paralyzed by the concerns of the past that we fail to see God's future.

Isaiah knew only too well that Israel's history was full of people who were willing to abandon the God they worshiped whenever their collective future seemed unclear. We, too, are tempted to abandon faith at the first sign of spiritual trouble! Our memories of the heartache of past sin tend to be incredibly short. When those wonderful religious experiences that have graced our lives come to an end and times of testing set in, and we're called to endure and then to mature, we are tempted to flee back in time to life before God, a time we remember mistakenly as a happier time. This is what Isaiah meant when he told the people, "Stop remembering the things you did in a former life. Stop entertaining all those fond notions about the things of old." Like Israel during the Exodus, we begin to wail about our lack of food and drink; and when Moses stays gone a little longer than we think he should, we quickly trade both him and our earrings in on a golden calf. Because Isaiah knew well the people he was dealing with, he warned them not to exchange the destiny of God's future for their own worthless past. "As we move into God's tomorrow, don't remember the things you once did. They have no life to them. Let them go."

Recognizing the difference between remembering the past and trying to reinhabit the past is an important distinction we need to learn to make ourselves. It is one thing to remember yesterday with fondness. It is quite another to try to dwell in those memories. Our Lord has done great things for us by freeing us from our bondage to nostalgia. For that we should be thankful. But now God has an even greater word to speak. Through Isaiah,

God is saying, "I am about to do a new thing among you. Even now it is springing forth before you! Look around you! Open your eyes! I'm building a highway in the wilderness! I'm planting rivers in the desert!" We need to hear this new word of hope.

Indeed, it is not just the false security of the past that beckons us; the concerns of the past may equally drain our energy and keep us from seeing God's future that Isaiah spoke about. Consider the hopelessness that has held our United Methodist Church paralyzed for so long. For thirty years we have been losing members. For thirty years we have been restructuring systems and fine-tuning programs and trying new corporate strategies to turn the tide. It has not worked. It has not worked because for thirty years we have acted in our own strength, even as we have moaned about our lack of life. It is time we had a prophet stand in our midst and tell us to quit fighting yesterday's battles. It is time we had a prophet offer us the good news of Jesus Christ by reminding us to gather, not in committees to debate the latest round of resolutions, but in worship to eat our one meal of Holy Eucharist. It is time somebody invited us to be faithful, not to the spirit of the age we inhabit, but to the covenant of the cross that saves.

If we somehow manage to hear this word, we will quit worrying about worldly success or churchly failure, or even the church's future. We won't be motivated by growth patterns or fiscal concerns. We will study God's Word rather than proclaim our own. We will live God's life and follow God's precepts, not ours. We will just try to be faithful. And the one sure sign of our faithful walk with God will be our return to the covenantal land of promise. No longer running after other gods who promise us other lands, we will settle down wherever we are and worship God in spirit and in truth (John 4:24).

This invitation to remember God faithfully has nothing to do with us dwelling in or escaping into our past. God is not resurrecting God's people so that they can relive their yesterdays or continue to fight old battles. God is offering us new life so that God may continue to love us and we may continue to be God's people. The divine invitation to live again is a call from God to come back home. So it was with Israel in exile. So it was with the prodigal in the pigsty. So it is with us.

Remembering is a communal, not a mental, act

If anybody had good reason to dwell in his own past, the apostle Paul did. His heritage was faultless, his practice perfect. But he also knew that his righteous acts meant nothing compared to the surpassing righteousness he had received freely from Christ. "Because of Christ," he said, "I now regard as loss all those good things I accomplished in former days."

Like Paul, Isaiah knew that God's people in any age need to set their minds firmly on God as they remember the mighty works God has begun among them already. Even though these works are still being crafted to perfection in us, we are prone to take them for granted. To counter our tendency to abandon God for the ways of our former life, Isaiah prefaced his new word by reminding Israel of the way God had made for them in the sea. He told how God had carved a path through the mighty waters just for them. It was a remarkable gift of new life to which they still owed their lives. It was a sign of God's favor that they still needed to acknowledge.

Developing the ability to discern God's new acts in our midst is not a mental discipline, though; nor do we learn it all by ourselves. It is a spiritual work we are taught to do by example in communities formed by grace. While God's righteousness is never granted to us as a reward for our good works, it is expressed in our lives by our good deeds. Gathering to remember, then, is central to our faithful worship. For when we struggle in the throes of spiritual death, one of the signs of our impending death is the failure of our memories. Left alone to fend for ourselves, we forget God's mighty acts of faithful care. But rehearsing the gracious acts of God within communities of faith rekindles our failing memories.

Though it was more than a dozen years ago now, I recall quite clearly the story of my grandfather's death. Lying non-responsively on what would soon be his death bed, my grandfather had receded in his mind to a place where no one could arouse him. Almost deaf, and almost a hundred years old, he had slipped beyond the reach of all who tried to offer him care. One morning, told that my grandfather was near death, one of his younger brothers arrived after driving several hundred miles to be with him. Sitting alone with him in his room, the younger brother held his hand and began speaking to him quietly in the Low-Dutch language they had spoken in their immigrant youth.

Throughout the morning, not even sure that his older brother could hear him, he continued to reminisce out loud, telling story after story about their parents, about the old homeplace where they had grown up, about the scenes of their childhood and the silly games they had once played. As he spoke of my grandfather's deceased wife and his many children, suddenly my dying grandfather began to stir. Pulled back, as it were, from the brink of death, he too began to chuckle and to tell stories in a language no one had spoken to him in many years. For a few short hours the years dropped away from those two elderly men, and they were once again brothers in the prime of their youth.

What I continue to find so amazing about this story is that contrary to all outward appearances, my grandfather's memory was fully intact. It had not been erased. It had not withered with the passage of time. All he needed was a mediator—a priest—to stir up the memories, and to be offered the right language in which to express himself. Both of these needs were supplied by his brother, who set him free from his present environs and enabled him to anticipate fully the future he was preparing already to inhabit.

Isaiah could not change the events that were swirling around Israel, but he could utter forth God's promise of a tomorrow beyond Assyria. "Open your eyes wide," he said, "for our God is about to accomplish a new thing among us. In fact, it is already starting. All appearances to the contrary, our future belongs not to Assyria but to God. Indeed, our God is already making for us a highway in the wilderness and planting new rivers in the desert!"

Isaiah's promise may not sound like a big deal to us, but it was amazing news to Israel. Every Israelite knew that the last time the Israelites as a people had passed through the wilderness, it had taken them forty long years to traverse a distance they should have covered in three days' march. They knew that a highway in the wilderness was a sign of God's favor, a seal of God's continued love. Assyria might take them away for a time, but when it was time to come home, God's highway would be completed. This new way would not only expedite their journey home, but it would graciously map out the way they were to go.

Similarly, the last time Israel had passed through the desert, the only water they had had to quench their thirst came from the miraculous tapping of Moses' rod against the rocks. Rivers in the desert, then, were another sure promise of God's merciful presence, a sign that God was already hard at work taking care of their tomorrows.

Re-membering is a gift that makes us one

These days we may know very little about Israel's troubles with Assyria, but we do know something about the covenant God has established with us in Christ Jesus. Like Isaiah long ago, there are prophets in our own time who are speaking faithfully the word of hope we need to hear. It is a word that teaches us that faithful memories can be shared only in congregations that gather. We may not always be excited about the prospects of fasting and praying and studying with our brothers and sisters in Christ. We may periodically get frustrated by a general lack of insight into our own spiritual darkness. But if we persist in being faithful on this life journey we are taking, we will gather with the family of faith and struggle against sin by remembering to call upon the Lord, who is always worthy to be praised. By faithfully committing Scripture to memory, we will not be so easily swayed by every wind of doctrine that blows along. Freed by God's Son and bathed in God's love and refashioned by God's Spirit, we will become living proof that there is no spirit of resignation in God. We will become part of God's "lived" answer to our world's resignation, for the very same God who once claimed an insignificant people called Israel has, in our baptism, laid a claim upon us, too.

Whether we were dunked in or dribbled on, it was in that grace-invested moment of baptismal drowning that death's power over us was broken forever. For in our baptism, we learn beyond doubt what lies beyond death. On the other side of death is not a grim reaper with face concealed, beckoning us irresistibly with bony finger to enter the frigid waters of the River Styx. On the far side of death, sitting on a throne from which flows a cleansing stream, is a loving God of light whose nail-pierced hands are reaching out to embrace us firmly and welcome us home.

Conclusion

Our world needs prophets like Isaiah who can recognize in the dismantling of our world the in-breaking of God's future. These prophets teach us that when we see the resignation building in people around us, it is time to speak of highways in the wilderness and of rivers in the desert, of old things passing away and all things becoming new.

This is why we insist on joining our hearts in worship and proclaiming with one voice, "Christ has died; Christ is risen; Christ will come again" ("A Service of Word and Table I," *The United Methodist Hymnal;* page 10). Every time we speak these words of mystery, we remember that Christ is God's truth and God's life. He is God's highway that leads our world out of the wilderness of its sin. He is God's river in our world's desert, a river of life that flows from the throne of God; and whoever drinks from him will never thirst again. The mystery of Christ is the good news our world needs desperately to hear! And we are the people God has called forth to proclaim it.

For a paralyzed church that for thirty years has groped for meaning to counter the darkness settling upon it, surely this is God's call on us. This is an invitation for us to come home. This is the word of resurrection we are longing to hear. God will not leave us without the witness of the Spirit. God will teach us all we need to know. God will empower us to do God's faithful will.

Let the church come together, then, and remember its faithful Christ!

We confess, O God, that we are too prone to forget your gracious way and too apt to remember our own way. Despite what your prophets advise, we do not want to gather with your people. We still think we can take this journey all by ourselves. As long as we can determine what happens tomorrow, we feel like we are still in control. We are not anxious to let your Spirit do its cleansing work in our lives.

Forgive us, we pray, for deciding for ourselves how we shall live. Make us a new people, that we might be free of our past. Make us a holy people, that we might honor you by our witness. Make us a loving people, that we might mirror the image of your blessed Son. Accept our lives, for we have nothing else we can offer you! Lord, in your mercy, hear our prayer.

7 Humility

Read: Isaiah 50:4-9a; Psalm 118:1-2, 19-29;
            Philippians 2:5-11; Luke 19:28-40

*O God of steadfast faith, who refused to abandon your Son to the grave, stand
by your people when we run after other gods who offer us other forms of faith.*
  *Purge from us our tendency to want to be great, that in our weakness we might
accept the joyous strength you offer in Jesus Christ, your blessed Son, our holy Lord,
who lives and reigns with you and the Holy Spirit, one God, in glory everlasting.
Amen.*

When we accept God's grace in Jesus, we begin a lifelong relationship
with our Lord that teaches us to delight in God's unchanging goodness.
But even though we are blessed by the holy presence of God, we quickly
discover that we are in constant need of divine help if we are to remain
faithful to God's covenant. Thanks be to God, then, that God, who is concerned to supply all our needs in Christ Jesus (Philippians 4:19), shares
with us four gifts that are indispensable to our spiritual well-being.

In order that we might not have to travel this path to perfection all by
ourselves, God places us in faith *communities* that predate us, that the
Spirit of God forms around us. Because there are times when we fail God
and choose to turn aside to the error of our own ways, God shares with us
regularly the gift of *reconciliation,* which we experience most fully in our
weekly meal of Holy Eucharist. Because there are other times when "this
world, with devils filled, should threaten to undo us" ("A Mighty Fortress
Is Our God," Martin Luther), God builds up our weak and fearful spirits
by giving us faithful *memories*, gathering us together to rehearse in worship God's mighty acts done on our behalf. Finally, because it often takes
a lifetime even for us who reside in the church to be freed of our culture's
infatuation with material success and victory, God models for us in Jesus
a fourth gift: *humility*. The sign of God's approval in our lives is not our
financial prosperity but our divinely-oriented identity. The holy promise
God shares with us does not bear the name *Nike*. It answers to the name
Emmanuel—"God with us."

For us today, this gift of humility may be the least appreciated of all
God's covenantal gifts. Even so, authentic discipleship is marked by a

humility of spirit, by a willingness to be in service to others, even a willingness to suffer at the hands of others. By his life and through his teachings, Jesus revealed to us that our God's glory has little to do with ruling over us like some despot. It expresses itself most clearly when it lies in lowly mangers and remains faithful to covenants promised, when it bows to wash feet and clings to wooden crosses. God desires to engender in us disciples of Christ that same divine spirit of meekness. Yet that desire will not be the sort of eye-catching theme that boosts worship attendance. Nor will it manifest itself in flashy programs that seek to entertain the great crowds looking for yet another diversion in life. It will, however, renew the face of the earth, for humility is the one gift that Jesus offers us that hallows our lives. It marks us with the sign of the cross and feeds us with the bread of new life. It is the fundamental building block of a new order of being, the being of Christ. It makes of us a gloriously new creation that does not grasp after glory but lives out our holy call in imitation of Jesus by taking up our own cross and giving our lives away.

Humility does not coexist with a triumphal attitude

We struggle greatly with the concept of self-denial today, primarily because we equate it simplistically with an ascetic lifestyle that is hopelessly out of vogue in a consumer-driven culture. But self-denial does not consist only of doing without those things we really want to have. In a society that is proud of rather than repentant about its overly-consumptive ways, learning to do without is surely important, but it is not all-important. Much more to the point are the words of John the Baptist, which teach us that the reason we practice self-decreasing is because Jesus is increasing (John 3:30).

When we are humble enough to deny ourselves, we are actually engaged in something much more positive and exciting than asceticism could ever be. Self-denial is an act that diverts our attention away from ourselves by turning our eyes upon Jesus. It re-forms us in the image of Jesus and clothes us with the servanthood of Christ, setting our transformed minds on things above (Colossians 3:2). It demands of us the lifelong admission that the only way we can become who we are to be is by accepting who Jesus is already. That is truly the heart of the matter. It is Jesus alone who clarifies for us what God's character is like and how we humans are to be. That means that disciples like us are charged by God to lose our old identities as we are changed by the Spirit of God into the likeness of our Lord.

Contrary to the blessed attitude of humility that God seeks to plant deep within us (Matthew 5:5) is the prosperity-centered attitude of our world, which clings desperately to the myth of upward mobility. Unfortunately, the church too has struggled against God's invitation to let go of this attitude.

This struggle shows itself clearly in the way we persist in interpreting the events of Palm Sunday. Despite the focus of our faith that teaches us to seek after humble service, we insist on calling Jesus' entry into Jerusalem a *triumphal* entry. Instead of seeing it as just one more step of faith—albeit an important step—in Jesus' own journey to the cross, we insist on believing that it is the manifestation of the glory of Christ. To be sure, it is always appropriate for us to lift our voices and sing with Saint Theodulph of Orleans, "All glory, laud, and honor, to thee, Redeemer, King" ("All Glory, Laud, and Honor," *The United Methodist Hymnal;* 280). But that does not give us license to celebrate Jesus' entry into Jerusalem in ways that encourage us to retain an unredeemed spirit of pride. And it surely is not the means we use to achieve eternal glory for ourselves. We have not yet grasped the spirit of this story if we insist on pointing to it as a way of saying, "See there! I told you that we could use this humility stuff to achieve personal greatness!"

While there is certainly cause for celebration in this event, it is not because Jesus suddenly reversed himself, set aside all the servant talk, and finally took Peter's advice on how to achieve lasting fame and glory (Matthew 16:22). Jesus' entry into Jerusalem shows us how faithful he remained to God, how seriously he continued to take his own baptismal calling. To the very end of his life, Jesus refused to take advantage of his equality with God. Instead, having taken upon himself our human nature, he humbled himself and became obedient, even to death on a cross. We celebrate Jesus' entry into Jerusalem, not because he flaunted his royalty for all to see, but because he chose to complete his earthly journey just as he had begun it—in utter humility. In imitation of Jesus, this is how humble we too are to be.

Taking another humble look at Jesus' entry into Jerusalem

Luke intentionally stripped Jesus' entry bare of all the images we associate with this event. There are no hosannas filling the air, no branches strewn along the way. There are no palms waved joyously or triumphantly. There is not a happy and swelling throng to make the entry look like a victory parade. There is not even an entry. By the end of our reading, our travelers have yet to even make it into the Holy City. What was Luke trying to tell us?

Like Peter long ago, we can speak on cue the language of humility; but we struggle to believe that Jesus is truly the humble Messiah he keeps telling us he is. Despite Luke's deliberate attempt to help us to see otherwise, we want a God who rules us with great authority, not one who serves us with tender compassion. Our popular perception of Jesus' entry is that it was a big deal, rather like what happens when the President arrives in his private jet. Briefed ahead of time, the press corps turns out to meet him. Cameras flash. Soldiers stand at attention. Red carpet lines the walks. Everyone is smiling and straining to see the President. But this popular perception of Jesus' entry is wrong.

Luke wanted us to realize that Jesus' entry into death in Jerusalem was like his entry into life in Bethlehem. There was no royal welcome either time, no imperial escort, no trumpeted fanfare. The man who had rejected earlier the messianic wishes of the Galilean crowd who had wanted to crown him king (John 6:15) refused even now to parade his royalty for all to see. Rather, the man who had taught his disciples that godly humility involves the rejection of worldly renown (Matthew 16:21) was now letting go of his own earthly life.

We may not want to let go of our own triumphalistic illusions about Jesus' entry, but the completion of our faith journey depends on it. Luke's version of our Lord's entry into Passover-clogged Jerusalem describes an event that went as unheralded then as our own attendance at a sporting event would be today.

Then, as now, people were arriving in droves, oblivious to everyone else as they made their way to the city gates. Once inside, first time attendees gawked at everything, excited just to be there. Those who had been there before were talking business or throwing private parties. Vendors hocked souvenirs. Food was being eaten in great quantities. The die-hard faithful were already purchasing lambs to sacrifice the next day. Roman police were roaming around, too, watching for rabble-rousers or other disturbers of the peace. Surrounded by everybody, the crowd was paying attention to nobody.

Arriving on the outskirts of the bustling city, Jesus was just one more unnamed pilgrim riding along an already overcrowded road. To his disciples he was a special man, an exceptional rabbi, the Son of God. But to everyone else he was one more face in a swarming throng of Jewish faithful gathering in the Holy City to celebrate the Passover.

By the time of Jesus, the Passover festival had already spanned some fifteen centuries. Participating in its hallowed acts reminded the people of their identity as God's people. The annual pilgrimage to their Holy City encouraged the Jews to tell their children the story of their faith (Deuteronomy 6:20-25), especially the journey their forebears had taken under cover of darkness when they stole out of Egypt one night. But with the passage of time, Passover had evolved into something more. No longer just a religious festival to the Jews, it had become a highly politicized event as well.

Except for a brief span of time under Hasmonean leadership, Israel had remained a petty puppet state under foreign rule for hundreds of years. Most recently, that foreign power had resided in Rome. The longer Israel languished in political servitude, the greater grew its own messianic hopes for a mighty ruler able to cast off the shackles of foreign domination. Because so much of its national identity was tied directly to the Passover, Israel had begun to expect its Messiah to appear at Passover as well. Since Israel insisted on congregating in Jerusalem to celebrate the Passover and to anticipate the arrival of its promised Messiah, Rome now chose to be there, too, watching and waiting alongside Israel.

As one might expect, the closer the pilgrims drew to Jerusalem, the more excited they became; and that made the Roman soldiers patrolling the streets of Jerusalem even more nervous and wary of the crowds gathering. They were determined not to allow any messianic-inspired disturbances to get out of hand. You won't find what I'm about to say in the history books, but I suspect that the Pharisees also stationed themselves on all the roads that led into Jerusalem. I know we think rather poorly of them, but the Pharisees were recognized leaders among the Jews of their day. They were pastoral figures who offered care and spiritual counsel to the Jewish populace. Out of concern that pilgrims not draw down the wrath of Rome on either themselves or the city, the Pharisees took it upon themselves to act as a kind of native crowd control during Passover. They warned the arriving pilgrims not to dance too wildly as they sang their arrival hymns (comprising Psalms 120–134), not to run in packs, not to taunt the soldiers.

The Pharisees intercepted Jesus and his disciples on the road that led from Jerusalem to Bethany, right where the path crested the Mount of Olives and started its descent to the Temple gate about a mile away. Contrary to what we typically assume, however, the Pharisees weren't overly concerned about Jesus. In fact, the men who actually talked with Jesus probably didn't have the first clue who he was. After all, this was the only trip to Jerusalem that Jesus the teacher ever took with his disciples.

The fact that the Pharisees referred to Jesus as a rabbi doesn't mean they recognized him. It was obvious he was traveling with a small band of disciples, as were other parties that were arriving. The Pharisees were simply being respectful when they called him Rabbi. That Jesus was riding a donkey was no big deal, either. Donkeys were the ancient equivalent of our modern taxi cabs. Hired out by owners to pilgrims who needed them, they could be rented along any of the routes that led into Jerusalem. When they saw this man bobbing along rather humorously astride a young donkey colt, the last thing these particular Pharisees would have had on their minds was an obscure messianic verse buried deep in the writings of the prophet Zechariah: "Shout aloud, O daughter Jerusalem! Lo, your king comes to you; . . . humble and riding on a donkey . . . " (9:9). In fact, John tells us that not even the disciples were aware of the links between Jesus' act and the words of the prophet (John 12:16). It wasn't until later, sometime after Jesus' death and subsequent resurrection, that they realized how much his entry into Jerusalem coincided with the prophet's vision of a gentle king.

Concerned only about the level of enthusiasm being exhibited by those in Jesus' party, the Pharisees told Jesus it would be a good idea to keep it down. In those days, Rome wasn't smiling so kindly on religious festivities that grew too festive! The disciples' praise of God needed to be more subdued. But Jesus would have none of it. To the Pharisees' well-meaning words of advice, he said, "If these men keep quiet now, the stones around us will begin to cry out." In their ignorant bliss, the disciples cheered their Rabbi's tart wit and danced an even more frenzied dance as a not-so-subtle in-your-face sort of response. In turn, the Pharisees probably cursed them all and said, "Stupid Galileans! This is exactly the kind of nonsense that will get us all in trouble!"

Humility involves our acceptance of God's will for us

Leaving the Pharisees behind, Jesus and his disciples continued down the steep decline until they saw the Holy City emerge into view through the trees. Then he broke down and wept. If this really were an entry of triumph, why would Jesus weep on the city's outskirts at the very moment of his greatest triumph? The answer lies in the open secret that Jesus' kingdom is not defined by the power and glory that the world seeks. I know we are reticent to accept this truth. That is why Luke stripped Jesus' entry into Jerusalem of all the sung hosannas and waved palm branches that symbolized the messianic glory Jesus had renounced.

Jesus' entry did not take place with pomp and pageantry. It occurred in gentle glory as our God revealed himself clearly in a stunning act of humility that elevated faithful love far above the exercise of raw strength. Willing to take up a cross that would kill him, Jesus wanted us, too, to come to terms with our own human brokenness and realize that God's power is made perfect in our weakness (2 Corinthians 12:9).

To be sure, whether we are the type of Christian who waves palms of glory in the presence of our Lord or the type who wears penitential ashes does not matter all that much. What does matter is whether we are faithfully discharging the call we have heard our Lord give us. For the goal of the Christian life is not that we triumph over the world by succeeding gloriously where it fails miserably. It is not that we amass great wealth (Luke 12:15-21) or that we reign as kings (Jeremiah 22:13-15a). It is that we learn to be in humble service to the world. It is that we become like Jesus, who had nowhere to lay his head (Matthew 8:20) and no one to speak in his defense. Strengthened in spirit to lay aside our own personal dreams of glory, we can finally quit harboring all those secret desires of triumphalism we have held on to for so long (Mark 10:35-37).

In a world that continues to worship fleeting celebrities as examples of success, we have the privilege of proclaiming the good news that we do not attain greatness in the eyes of God by notching victories or earning millions. Greatness has to do with becoming least, with growing humble, with embracing a *downwardly*-mobile theology and looking more and more like our servant Lord. One of the results of this new way of living is that we finally realize how foolish it is for us to repackage Jesus so that he will look more attractive to nations that are bent on consuming everything in sight. Recasting Jesus in images our world already accepts will not make him more attractive to anyone. It will only render him dispensable to everyone.

If the parable of the ten talents that Jesus told just prior to his entry into Jerusalem (Luke 19:11-27) provides any sort of interpretive guidance to his act, then Jesus didn't enter Jerusalem as a king expecting to be crowned. He came as a loyal Son determined to carry out his Father's will, even if it cost him his life. Indeed, his only purpose in entering the city was to leave it. As in the parable he told, Jesus was preparing to exit this world. Like the nobleman, Jesus was completing the last steps necessary to take the journey he had been told to take at the time of his transfiguration.

Remember? Back on the mountain when he was transfigured, Jesus had a conversation with Moses and Elijah. They talked that day about his exodus from Jerusalem, not his entry into Jerusalem (Luke 9:31). From that moment forward, like the nobleman in his story, Jesus had been preparing to leave Jerusalem behind. He had heard clearly the call that had come from the far country of heaven, informing him that it was time to be crowned King. Because of his infinite love for the servants he would soon be leaving behind, it was time for Jesus to entrust the care and maintenance of his coming Kingdom to us, his servants, the church—the disciples he had called. Offering the disciples his peace, and advising them to use faithfully the community-building gifts his blessed Spirit would be sharing with them soon, Jesus left.

In his absence, some of us are proving to be reliable servants, using the gifts of the Spirit in faithful ways that bring honor to the name of Jesus. Others of us are using the gifts we have been given to administer merciful justice on his behalf. Some of us, however, are choosing to disregard his gifts, afraid to use them, saving them back for who knows what reason. Still others of us are refusing even to be his servants, choosing instead to remain his subjects, an unhappy people who are frustrated that God has chosen such a humble figure to be crowned our King eternal. The day is surely approaching, though, when he will return as King of kings and Lord of lords and claim for his own the kingdom he has inherited from his Father. When that time comes, he will ask if we have lived as he did. He will ask if we lived our lives with humility.

Conclusion

The gift of humility that God shares with us does not guarantee that we will become worldly successes or powerful agents of change. Humility is the compass Jesus offers us that enables us to grow faithful in spirit. It makes it possible for us to follow wherever Jesus leads us and to receive with gratitude God's will for our lives, even when that destiny tastes bittersweet to the world in which we live. It frees us from our bondage to ourselves and allows us to pour out our lives in gentle, self-denying service to the world, just as Jesus has done for us, because he told us to do this in remembrance of him.

Changed over time into the likeness of Christ, we disciples of Jesus are in the process even now of becoming a holy people who live faithfully, just as Jesus lived. Like our Lord, we have been called to serve, not to succeed. We have been cleansed to love, not to control. We have been empowered to shine forth as lights to the nations, not to rule as petty monarchs over them. We have been invited to give our lives away. Thanks be to God that in Christ we can finally let go of all our old worldly aspirations. The gift of humility entitles us, like Jesus before us, to worship our God with selfless joy and to serve our neighbors with righteous conviction.

Let us greet our faithful Christ with cries of, "Hosanna in the highest!"

We confess, O God, that we are not yet a humble people. We fight openly for our rights but forget to lift up one another in prayer, even in secret. We work hard to make our homes comfortable to us but fail to share your compassion with others. We enjoy our leisure too much to labor for your coming Kingdom. We act as if we are somehow your equals, not children you have formed in your image and redeemed with your love.

Forgive us, we pray, for thinking more highly of ourselves than we should. Grant us a spirit of obedience, that we might learn true humility. Empty yourself into us, that we might receive your righteousness. Offer to us your pardon, that we might grow into your likeness. For blessed is your Son who comes in the name of the Lord! Lord, in your mercy, hear our prayer.

Epilogue

We began this journey committed to taking the Christian faith seriously again. We wanted to learn what Christians believe. We wanted to hear what God expects of us. We wanted to know what a life of faith would be like.

To accomplish this task, we have paused along the way to consider seven crucial aspects of the Christian faith. We looked first at the topic of *repentance* and realized that the Spirit of Christ desires to teach us new ways to live that counter those we have been taught by the world. We learned that our repentance has been made possible by the gracious gift of forgiveness that God has spoken in the life, death, and resurrection of Jesus.

We have also learned that this path to righteousness is not trouble free. However, blessed by God's presence and thankful for God's faithfulness, we have been encouraged to face courageously the *temptations* that threaten our new identities in Christ. Realistic concerns about whether we would have the spiritual stamina necessary to overcome these threats led us next to consider the faithfulness of God and the *covenant* God has made with us.

Finally, we discovered that in order to establish God's covenant in our lives so that it could generate faith within us, God has shared with us four additional facets of grace. While we have isolated these gifts from one another in order to analyze them more carefully, the gifts of *community, reconciliation, memory*, and *humility* are actually inseparable. Through them, God offers to us pilgrims an interrelated network of grace, support, and counsel.

Because God shares these gifts with us in abundance, we have learned that we can be faithful on this walk. As we mature into the faith of the church, we can become one with Christ, who makes all this possible by his selfless offer of love. In turn, we too can "offer ourselves in praise and thanksgiving as a holy and living sacrifice, in union with Christ's offering for us" ("A Service of Word and Table I," *The United Methodist Hymnal;* page 10).

Now it is time to profess openly the faith commitments we have made along the way. Some of us have found Christ in these pages. Some of us have emerged from this journey with a greater appreciation for God's faithful people. Some of us have decided that this is not the path we wish to take.

What our world now needs from those of us who have agreed to bear the name of Christ is faithful adherence to our Lord. The world needs to see faithful pilgrims determined to follow Jesus at any cost. It needs to hear Christ's faithful words proclaimed against the trifling assumptions our culture makes. Thanks be to God! For these are precisely the needs that God has already supplied us in Christ Jesus!

Study Guide

A Word to the Leader

Thank you for assuming the awesome responsibility of guiding the class through this study. As leader, you have the privilege of helping participants find insights in these pages that will transform their lives and deepen their commitments to Christ.

As you prepare to take up the responsibility and the privilege of leading this class, read the Study Guide carefully. It contains step-by-step guidance for each session. The topics contained in the seven chapters are designed to appeal to both head and heart. Therefore, the questions and suggestions in the Study Guide provide opportunities for both further study and practical application of insights gained. Feel free to adapt the questions and suggestions to meet the needs of your class.

There may well be people in your class who are either unfamiliar with or new to the Christian faith. Be sensitive to their needs. At times you may need to provide historical background for some of the biblical stories (for example, the Exodus or the Exile) to create a larger context for the discussion. At other times you may need to take extra time to explain key biblical words or theological terms.

The seven-chapter format makes the book an ideal small-group study for use during Lent. However, it may be used with profit at any time of the year. You may also vary the length of the study; it certainly does not have to be completed over a seven-week period. Be sensitive to the needs and interests of your group as you decide these matters.

An important goal of this book is to allow the Holy Spirit to begin a work of transformation in the life of every reader—including you, the leader. Our prayer is that as you prepare for class and as you lead your group, you will begin to look and act more and more like Jesus and less and less like the culture around you. May the members of your group, through your leadership, find Christ and thus find life so that they may begin to know how to live as Christians in a non-Christian world.

CHAPTER 1
Repentance
(pp. 7–14)

1. Begin the class session (and all class sessions) with prayer. You may want to use the prayer provided on page 7. Encourage the class to adopt the habit of praying daily the prayer that begins the chapter they are presently studying.

2. Explain the importance of reading and reflecting upon the scriptural lessons listed at the beginning of each chapter. (The theological positions of the church are based upon Scripture. Also, the topics discussed in each chapter arise out of the lessons listed.)

   If your pastor preaches regularly from the Revised Common Lectionary found in *The United Methodist Book of Worship*, inform the class that the scriptural lessons for the chapters in this book are the lessons for Sunday worship during the season of Lent, Year C. This connection with Lent is important for the overall focus of the book, for Lent has historically served the church as a time of instruction for those interested in becoming Christians, or as a time of reclamation of those who have drifted—or fallen—away from the faith but want to take their faith seriously once again.

3. This first chapter has two purposes:
   - It interprets the place and importance of repentance in the life of Christians. It does this in a variety of ways. For instance, it offers a way to relate confession to repentance. Or, based on Jesus' sermon in Matthew 6, it suggests three acts—almsgiving, prayer, and fasting—that we can perform that keep repentance from being something we did once in our past and make it a present reality that expresses our new identities in Jesus.
   - It serves as a wake-up call to the Christian community to remember that God re-creates the people of God by making them into a holy, or set-apart, people. It issues this call by insisting that we subject the claims of our culture to the scrutiny of our faith.

   As you plan your lesson, you will need to decide which of these two discussion tracks on repentance you and your class will pursue.

4. If you choose the first alternative, help your class understand how Christian belief in repentance should produce in us a new life of

thanksgiving to God, not additional feelings of guilt and shame. Otherwise, repentance is not a word of gospel (good news)!

Use the following questions to guide your class discussion:

- What thoughts come to mind when you hear the word *repentance*?
- What feelings do you associate with repentance: joy? guilt? shame? hostility? Explain your answer.
- What is the relationship between confession and repentance? (If necessary, provide a short definition of each. Confession is the admission of wrong and the acceptance of personal responsibility. Repentance is a lifestyle of thanksgiving to God that finds expression in ongoing acts like fasting, prayer, and almsgiving.)
- Does your church invite you to confess sin on a regular basis as an act of worship?
- If so, do you confess before or after the sermon? Does the place of confession in worship matter? Why? Why not?
- Does your pastor speak words of absolution (forgiveness) after you confess? Why are words of absolution important? (The point of confession is to be done with sin, not to wallow in it.)
- Do you hear the fact that we are already forgiven as a word of gospel grace? Does God's forgiveness enable you to live for Jesus? Does it offer you spiritual license to do as you please without fear of reprisal?
- What acts do you perform regularly to express your repentance? Can you describe these acts as the giving of alms, as prayer, or as fasting? What would help you to take these three acts more seriously or to perform them more regularly?

5. If you choose the second alternative, prepare ahead of time a list of popular ideas, slogans, claims, and teachings that deny the possibility, and thus the reality, of repentance. Use the following questions to guide your class discussion:
   - In what ways have your actions and comments from yesterday continued to determine how you act or speak today? Do you feel powerless to control the ways you behave or speak? Why? Why not? How have you tried to overcome the influence of your past?
   - How do the human sciences such as psychology or sociology encourage us to disregard our Christian faith as a reputable source for learning how to live as human beings? How do cultural institutions like public schools, the medical field, insurance, and business (for example, credit cards) turn us away from Christ?
   - What methods does our culture use to teach us to live with ourselves? Do these methods help? Do they aggravate the situation?

- Are guilt and shame ever good things? How? When? Distinguish between *feeling* guilty and *being* guilty.
- How can the church help us recognize the difference between false feelings of shame and Spirit-induced pangs of conscience?

6. For those in the class who are ready to take deliberate steps toward being formed in the Christian faith, offer either of these two options:
   - Invite the class members to form small groups of no more than five or six people. If you used the discussion time to consider the place of repentance in the Christian life, ask the groups to meet weekly to practice acts of repentance. These groups should not only hold each other accountable but should also hold each other up in prayer in regard to the acts of repentance selected.
   - Invite the class members to form small groups of no more than five or six people. If you used the discussion time to talk about cultural denials of repentance, ask the groups to meet weekly to discuss particular topics in *The Book of Resolutions of The United Methodist Church* or the "Social Principles" in *The Book of Discipline of The United Methodist Church*. This is a deliberate act that will encourage class members to act toward and think about societal issues from a confessional Christian stance.

7. Instruct the class to prepare for the next class session by reading Chapter 2 and the Scripture passages listed at the beginning of Chapter 2. You may want to designate someone in the class to lead the prayer of confession and to speak the words of forgiveness (absolution) when you next meet.

   Remind your class that the purpose of this study is not just to acquire a few facts about faith. It is to be formed in faith and to become more faithful. Thus, the regular reading of the scriptural lessons and the offering of the prayers in each chapter are just as important as the classroom discussions.

8. Invite your class to pray at the conclusion of each day the prayer of confession at the end of the chapter they are studying. Conclude today's session by praying the prayer of confession on page 14.

   Following the prayer of confession, allow one or two minutes of silence for personal reflection, private confession, and examination of conscience. Then invite the class to speak responsively these words of comfort and forgiveness:
   LEADER: In the name of Jesus Christ, your sins are forgiven!
   CLASS: In the name of Jesus Christ, your sins are forgiven, too!

CHAPTER 2
Temptation
(pp. 15–22)

1. Begin the class by praying the prayer on page 15. After the prayer, ask your class how praying this prayer each day since you last met together has helped or hindered their spiritual focus. Encourage the class members to use the prayer in their daily devotional time.

2. Remind the class of the importance of reflecting upon the scriptural lessons. You may want to ask if Chapter 2 helped make sense of the readings at the beginning of the chapter. If it did not, ask what the class members would have preferred that the chapter discuss.

    If you are reading this chapter during the season of Lent, invite your class to discuss why the Gospel reading on the first Sunday in Lent always focuses on the temptations of Jesus. (You may want to ask your pastor to explain the origin, symbolism, and purpose of the forty days of Lent.)

    Before the session, assign one of the class members the task of comparing the temptation scenes in each of the Gospel accounts and sharing with the class how the scenes are similar and different. (The order of the temptations varies in Matthew and Luke; Mark mentions the fact of temptation but doesn't tell us what the temptations were; John doesn't mention the temptations at all.)

3. The purpose of Chapter 2 is threefold.
    *   It helps us face squarely the place of temptation in our lives. Indeed, the closer we draw to Christ, the more real temptation will become.
    *   It invites us to take temptation seriously by realizing how subtle it can be.
    *   It tries to convince us that, just as Christ recognized and overcame temptation in his life, we can, too, in our lives.

    Decide whether to structure your discussion time around either life issues or theological themes. These are not hard and fast distinctions, but the first approach is more practical and the second is more academic.

4. If you select the option of life issues, use the following questions to guide your discussion:
    *   Are you more comfortable talking about a personal devil or imper-

sonal evil as the primary source of temptation? Explain.

- As a source of temptation, is there a difference between the devil and the world (or our culture)?
- Do you struggle more with temptations for *big* sins or for *little* sins? How would you distinguish between them?
- What or where is Egypt in your life? What or where is the wilderness into which the Spirit of God has called you?
- Describe how you have triumphed over or fallen prey to the temptations you have experienced in the wilderness.
- Can communities, like individuals, be tempted to sin? If so, offer some examples. (Examples may include national issues such as slavery or abortion, local issues such as city council rulings or neighborhood decisions, or church issues such as missional practices or church council policies.)
- Have you been told that giving your life to Jesus would solve all your problems? Has it? Has it created new problems? If it has created new problems or made some existing problems worse, how did you reconcile this reality with the words you were told? Did you ever think that there was something wrong with you because your experience was so different from what you were told?
- Does your church believe that faith "must be formed in you"? If so, how does your church try to form the faith in people? (Examples include classes for baptism, confirmation, or membership; DISCIPLE Bible studies; *Covenant Discipleship* groups; *Walk to Emmaus* reunion groups.)
- In relation to temptation, is the distinction between the work of God and the word of God helpful? How have these been played off against each other in your life?

5. If you select the option of theological themes, use the following questions to guide your discussion:
   - Do we really believe that Jesus was "truly human"? What are we saying when we join our voices to that of the church and profess the Nicene Creed (*The United Methodist Hymnal*, 880)?
   - Do we sometimes cite Jesus' divinity to excuse our own sinfulness ("Sure, Jesus was sinless. But he was God! We're just human . . .")?
   - Do we really believe that Jesus could have sinned? Why or why not? What difference does it make theologically?
   - Did Jesus have to overcome temptation the same way we do, relying on God, trusting the Holy Spirit? Explain.
   - What is the difference between temptation and sin? At what point

does temptation become sin? (Remind the class that a discussion of temptation and sin is provided on pages 17 and 18. Possible definitions of temptation include "the invitation to discard our new identity in Christ," "to take advantage of our relationship with God," "to commit an activity that denies our relationship with Christ." Sin is the acceptance of this invitation or the commission of the deed.)

- Give some examples of how temptation has challenged your identity or encouraged you to take advantage of your relationship with God.
- How has the Spirit of God helped you to discern when you were being tempted?
- Is evil "hopelessly unimaginative"? If so, what does this say about church committees that respond regularly with comments such as, "That's not the way we do things around here"?
- In your experience, or in your opinion, has the church been guilty of encouraging us to treat our salvation, our new identities in Christ, as a privilege to exploit as opposed to a call to servanthood (to be a light to the nations)? Do we, by our prayers or otherwise, sometimes treat God as a genie we can summon to act on our whims? (Use some of the examples suggested on page 19, for example expecting God to provide us with a new job or a parking place; or tell your own story.)

6. For those in the class who are ready to take deliberate steps toward being formed in their Christian faith, offer the following options for prayer:
   - Pray for your pastor. Pastors are often tempted to leave behind congregations that have problems or seem unappreciative, thinking they are being called to a new congregation.
   - Pray for your classmates, especially if they are young Christians. Sometimes Christians are shocked to discover that not everyone in the church is taking his or her faith seriously or is interested in growing spiritually. This realization can be a temptation to decide that faith is an illusion.
   - Pray for the world, especially for those who have not yet heard the good news that Jesus has broken the power of sin in our lives. Covenant together to tell someone this good news this week.

7. Tell the class to read Chapter 3 and the Scripture passages listed at the beginning of Chapter 3. Designate someone to lead the prayer of confession and to speak the words of forgiveness at the close of the next class session.

8. Conclude your class session by praying the prayer of confession on

page 22. Remember to give the members of the class plenty of time to pray silently and to examine their conscience. You (or the person designated in the last class session) should then speak words of comfort and forgiveness to the class. Invite the class to say responsively:

LEADER: In the name of Jesus Christ, your sins are forgiven!

CLASS: In the name of Jesus Christ, your sins are forgiven, too!

CHAPTER 3
Covenant
(pp. 23–30)

1. Begin your class by praying the prayer on page 23. After the prayer, ask your class these questions:
   - In what ways is your prayer life deepening?
   - Does your church encourage you to pray? How? Does it take prayer for granted?
   - How could your church better nurture your class in the life of prayer?

2. Remind the class of the importance of reflecting upon the scriptural lessons. You may want to ask if this chapter has helped to make sense of the readings at the beginning of the chapter. If not, ask what the class members would have preferred that the chapter discuss.

   If your pastor preaches from the Revised Common Lectionary, or if you are reading this text during the season of Lent, you may want to tell the class that each week of Lent during Year B, the Old Testament lessons read during Sunday worship discuss the various covenants that God formed with the people of Israel. Specifically mentioned in the Year B readings are those covenants made with Noah, Abraham, Moses (twice), and Jeremiah.

   Explain the meaning of *covenant*. A covenant is a divine promise. If the class is unclear about what God's covenant with the church today is, explain that it is the promise of salvation in Jesus Christ. This promise includes both the release from sin and the offer of holiness.

3. Chapter 3 has two purposes:
   - It confronts our culture's identification of personal well-being with God's saving offer of covenant, suggesting that they are not the same thing.
   - It creates a bridge between life in our world and the divine gifts that God shares with us. Were it not for God's covenant, for instance, we would not be able to live as Christians. Were it not for the four gifts of community, reconciliation, memory, and humility, God's covenant would be too exacting for most of us to fulfill.

   As you plan your lesson, you will probably need to focus your attention on either the general human problem of spiritual struggle or the divine solution of covenant. You will have time to combine the two ideas in an effective way only if your class meets for more than an hour at a time or is spreading these lessons over more than one class session.

4. If you decide to focus on the issue of spiritual struggle, use these questions to guide your discussion:
   - Are sermons that promise us self-fulfillment at odds with the gospel? If so, why?
   - Can you think of advertising jingles that are contrary to the gospel? (A starter list might include "You only go around once in life"; "You deserve a break today"; "Because there's only one you.") Discuss.
   - What is the difference between a word that builds us up and one that puffs us up? (See Ephesians 4:7-16.)
   - How have you handled those times when you prayed for something (physical health, a job, a healed relationship) and it did not happen? Did you blame God? Did you assume that the problem lay with you? How did you ultimately resolve the hurt involved?
   - Have you been hurt deeply by someone in the church? How did you deal with the break in the relationship? If no reconciliation occurred between you and the other person(s), how did you work through the pain? How did you deal with the ensuing doubts and spiritual struggle? (If class members respond openly and honestly to this question, it may be necessary to pause the discussion and offer up their hurts to God. Invite everyone to hold hands as the class offers prayer for the people in pain. Encourage two or three class members who are close to the people or feel led by God's Spirit, to offer short prayers of intercession.)

5. If you decide to focus on God's covenant, use these questions to guide your discussion:
   - If you were Abraham, how would you have responded to the promise that God kept repeating to you over a span of some twenty-five years?
   - How long are you willing to wait in vain for a spouse, friend, or colleague to make good on a promise before you cease to believe what the person is telling you?
   - How do you determine when an offer of job advancement that requires geographical relocation to another city is really a temptation to break covenant with God? Have you ever known someone who refused a promotion because it would interfere with or render impossible to fulfill her covenant at church to "faithfully participate

in its ministries by your prayers, your presence, your gifts, and your service" ("The Baptismal Covenant Service I," *The United Methodist Hymnal;* © 1976, 1980, 1985, 1989 The United Methodist Publishing House; Used by permission; page 38)? Have you ever stayed home from work on Friday so that you would be physically well enough to go to church on Sunday? (These questions are intended to help class members think deeply about which of the various covenants in their lives they keep, which they break, and why. If their covenant with God is broken regularly or always ends up playing second fiddle to the other covenants of life, the discussion could turn to what your church needs to be doing to strengthen its disciples to take their covenant with God more seriously.)

- Have you ever participated in "Wesley's Covenant Service"? What was your reaction to the covenant prayer and its demands on your life? Did it encourage you to try to become more faithful? Did it remind you that God is always present, enabling you to be more faithful? (A copy of "Wesley's Covenant Service" can be found in *The United Methodist Book of Worship,* pages 291–294. If no one in your class has ever participated in this worship service, ask your pastor to offer the service on New Year's Eve, as a prayerful response to the Word on a Sunday morning, at a prayer vigil on Easter Eve, or on a Wednesday evening in place of the regular Bible study or prayer time.)

6. Remember that these chapters (and the Study Guide section that corresponds to each chapter) are designed to *form* as much as to *inform* disciples. A good class discussion always remains secondary to the work of the Spirit. As the Spirit works within the class members who are listening carefully and reading intently, be sensitive pastorally to those moments when the discussion leads an individual into a moment of truth, or the entire class into a time of disclosure. You do not need to fear these moments, for God will guide you as you prayerfully lead the class; but neither do you want to treat these moments as intrusions that have gotten the discussion "off course."

7. Invite class members who are ready to take additional steps toward being formed in their Christian faith to join with three or four others in the class and write a spiritual covenant that they promise to keep. The covenant should include a specific act or two based on each of the four vows (prayers, presence, gifts, service) made at the time one joins the church (see *The United Methodist Hymnal,* page 38). To promote accountability, the group should meet weekly to discuss how

participants kept—or why they broke—their covenant. Be sure they understand that they are meeting together for mutual encouragement, not for rebuke or discipline.

8. Remind the class to read Chapter 4 and the Scripture passages listed at the beginning of Chapter 4. Designate a class member to lead the prayer of confession and to speak the words of forgiveness at the next session. Additional prayers of confession and acts of pardon can be found in *The United Methodist Book of Worship* (475–494). You may want to share these resources with the person you designate.

9. Conclude your class session by offering the prayer of confession on page 30. Remember to allow the class plenty of time for silent prayer and examination of conscience. Invite the class to speak responsively these words of comfort and forgiveness:
   LEADER: In the name of Jesus Christ, your sins are forgiven!
   CLASS: In the name of Jesus Christ, your sins are forgiven, too!

CHAPTER 4
Community
(pp. 31–39)

1. Begin your class by praying the prayer on page 31. Ask the members of the class how praying daily the prayers at the beginning and end of each chapter is affecting their lives.

2. To open this session, you may want to spend some time talking about prayer. If members of the class are struggling with written prayers, as opposed to extemporaneously-spoken prayers, it may be helpful to share some of the following ideas about prayer:

    *   Extemporaneous prayer is a fairly recent innovation in the church. When Wesley began to experiment with extemporaneous prayer, he was chastised by both priests and laypeople who were shocked by his "disregard" for the accepted prayer forms of the church.

    *   Jesus' disciples asked Jesus to teach them to pray. Since we are no wiser theologically nor any more faithful to Jesus than they were, we should not be too proud to allow the community of faith into which Jesus has placed us, to teach us to pray.

    *   For almost three thousand years, the Book of Psalms has been the prayer book of both the Jews and the church. In these prayers we learn how to pour out to God our feelings of sorrow in lamentful prayers and our shouts of praise in hearty song.

    *   Hymnals are the church's Spirit-led addition to the Psalms. Hymns are often prayers of the people that have been set to music so that we do not forget them. They are excellent models that teach us how to pray.

    *   Devotional pamphlets such as *The Upper Room* and books by authors such as Oswald Chambers are full of written prayers. So, too, is our *Hymnal.* (An index to all the prayers that appear in *The United Methodist Hymnal* can be found in *The United Methodist Book of Worship*, page 497).

    *   Because there are times when we do not know how to pray (see Romans 8:26), and other times when we are either too ill or too busy or too full of fear to pray extemporaneously, the Spirit who intercedes for us can bring to our mind prayers we have memorized.

3. If corporate prayers of confession are not prayed regularly in your church, there may be class members who fail to understand why they

need to pray this type of prayer. They may say things like, "I admit that those things are sinful, but I'm not guilty of them. Why should I confess them?"

Without arguing for or against our communal solidarity, use the question as an opportunity to pair mentors with younger Christians in your class in order to teach them the importance of corporate prayers.

If you need help in explaining the importance of corporate prayers, ask your pastor to give you an explanation, to meet with your class briefly at the end of the class period, or to suggest church library resources on prayer that class members might read.

4. Chapter 4 has three purposes:
    - To speak candidly of our need to submit our lives to Christ, who inhabits the saints who populate the church.
    - To make clear that Christians are always a communally-gathered people, not a loose collection of discrete individuals.
    - To realize that becoming like Christ does not happen immediately. It takes both time and saintly models. Our *formation* as Christians involves much more than the *information* we received when we joined the church.

    As you plan your lesson, focus your attention on either the issue of our submission to Christ through the community of faith, or the issues of confrontation and discipline that arise in communities.

5. If you decide to explore issues that arise out of our submission to the community of faith, use these questions to guide your discussion:
    - If your congregation uses mentors (Christians who are mature in faith and serve as faith guides for young Christians), who chooses them? Are there qualifications they must meet? If so, what are the qualifications? Who sets them? Are mentors "commissioned" by your local church? To whom are they assigned? How long are they paired with young Christians?
    - If your church does not use mentors, why not? Is trust—or distrust— an issue? Has using mentors been tried before? How do young Christians learn about the faith if they are not paired with someone who is already faithful?
    - How do we submit our individual needs to the concerns of the community of faith? When is this submission appropriate? When is it inappropriate? Why are we so hesitant about being submissive?
    - Respond to the author's conclusion: "I come to God holding your hand, or I don't come at all" (page 38). Is a "Jesus and me" attitude

contrary to the Christian faith? Why? Why not?

6. If you decide to explore issues of discipline, confrontation, and political involvement that can wreak havoc in communities of faith, use the following questions to guide your discussion:

   • How are errant members disciplined in your church? Are their sinful actions ignored? Do other members learn to avert their eyes and pretend these incidents didn't happen? Do you deny that anything sinful has occurred? If discipline is offered, what forms does it take? Is it effective? Who decides the type or degree of discipline? Do members submit to discipline, or do they join other churches or just leave?

   • What does it mean to say that God will not allow us to be tempted beyond what we can bear? If this is true, why do so many people fall prey to temptation? What personal experiences would you be willing to share with the other members of the class?

   • How does your church handle confrontation? How do you reconcile conflict with other members? What guidelines does our faith offer to assist Christians in addressing our problems faithfully? (See Matthew 18:15-20.)

   • How does the church determine its role in society? How does it arbitrate among competing truth claims within the church or among various interpretations of a passage of Scripture? How does the church decide what to think about social issues such as the death penalty, abortion, or divorce? (Submitting the issue to a study based on Scripture, tradition, reason, and experience, commonly referred to as the Wesleyan quadrilateral, is one possible approach.) Does The United Methodist Church have an official stance on topics like these? How has the church arrived at these positions? How does your local church adopt guidelines that assist you in your Christian walk?

7. For class members who are ready to take additional steps toward being formed in their Christian faith, offer the following two options:

   • Encourage those who are mature in their faith to be spiritual mentors. Encourage them to "adopt" a child, a teen, or another adult. Information on how to proceed as a mentor is readily available in confirmation materials. See also the resources listed on page 96. Speak with your pastor ahead of time about the possibility of providing mentors for people joining the church, for people at the time of their baptism or confirmation, or even for committees or Sunday school classes.

   • Encourage those who are new to the Christian faith, or who are beginning to take their faith seriously, to ask for a mentor who will guide them in matters of Christian action and formation.

8. Tell the class to read Chapter 5 and the Scripture passages listed at the beginning of Chapter 5. Designate someone to lead the prayer of confession and to speak the words of forgiveness at the close of the next class session.

9. Conclude your class session by praying the prayer of confession on pages 38 and 39. During the time of silent prayer and examination of conscience, invite class members to pray that your local church may become a community that instructs the faithful, accepts the sinful, cares for the broken, disciplines the prodigal, and worships with integrity and joy. Then invite the class to speak responsively the following words of comfort and forgiveness that assure the class of God's love:
LEADER: In the name of Jesus Christ, your sins are forgiven!
CLASS: In the name of Jesus Christ, your sins are forgiven, too!

CHAPTER 5

Reconciliation

(pp. 40–48)

1. Begin your class by praying the prayer on page 40 or by inviting one of the class members to offer his or her own prayer. Remind the class to pray the printed prayer regularly throughout the week.

2. The purpose of this chapter is to help class members realize that, given our fallen status, believers will sin. However badly our sin may hurt God, though, it will not make God hate us. God has made provisions to receive us back into the fellowship of believers we call the church. We call this divine gift of love reconciliation. Because God shares reconciliation with us, we can learn to share it with one another, too.

    As you plan your lesson, focus your attention on either the issues surrounding reconciliation in the local church, or the theology of our meal of Holy Eucharist (the Lord's Supper).

3. If you choose to explore issues surrounding the gift of reconciliation in the local church, use the following questions to guide your discussion:
    *   In case anyone misunderstood the pun on page 41 about there never being any excuse for sin but "always justification for it," explain that the reference is to the justifying faith we obtain in Christ (see Galatians 2:16). No one ever becomes so prodigal or drifts so far away from faith that God can't reach him or redeem her.
    *   Do you have a time called "passing the peace" that occurs after, and as a response to, the sermon in your worship service? If so, do members in the congregation use this time to reconcile differences and hurts with one another, or do they say hello to one another? If you do not have a time like this in worship, how and when do people in the congregation reconcile with one another? What are the advantages or disadvantages to making our offering of reconciliation a regular part of our weekly worship?
    *   Are you more comfortable talking about salvation in terms of "getting saved" or "coming home"? Why? Does the terminology used to describe the event affect your experience of the event?
    *   How does your congregation deal with and/or reach out to the prodigal elder children who remain within the church but do not share in its joy?

- How does your congregation handle prodigal younger children who leave when times are tough but return when a new preacher is appointed? Is forgiveness offered or withheld? Why? Why not?

4. If you choose to explore the theology of our meal of Holy Eucharist, use the following questions to guide your discussion:
   - In how many different ways have members of this class shared the meal of Holy Communion? (A partial list might include kneeling at the chancel or altar rail, sitting in groups of twelve around a table, standing in a line that processes to the Table, sitting in the pews as the bread and wine are passed like offering plates.) How many of these forms have been practiced in your local church? Which do you prefer? Why?
   - What are some of the names the church uses for this sacrament? (A partial list would include the Lord's Supper, the Last Supper, Holy Eucharist, Holy Communion, the Mass.) What aspect of the meal is highlighted by each name that we call it? (Lord's Supper—the messianic banquet that is still to come; Last Supper—the memorial meal of Maundy Thursday; Holy Eucharist—the thanksgiving of praise; Holy Communion—the meal of fellowship; Mass—the sacrificial nature of Christ's offering)
   - When you eat the meal of Holy Eucharist, do you approach it as a solemn time in which you remember the death of Jesus? Do you approach it in joy as a time of celebration when you anticipate the time when "Christ comes in final victory and we feast at his heavenly banquet" ("A Service of Word and Table I," *The United Methodist Hymnal;* page 10)? Why?
   - Can you explain how Jesus is present in the meal? (Three standard explanations include (1) Transubstantiation—the bread and wine change into the body and blood of Christ; (2) Consubstantiation—Christ is spiritually present in, with, and under the bread and wine; (3) Memorial—Christ is not "present" in the meal; we simply think about Jesus while we eat. These positions are much more complex than described here. Most theological dictionaries have an entry for the Lord's Supper that offers a more nuanced explanation.)

5. If there are those in the class who are ready to take additional steps in the formation of their faith, offer one or more of the following options in regard to Holy Eucharist:
   - Invite your pastor to share a theology of the sacraments. Ask the pastor to be prepared to discuss the following issues:

1) What is a sacrament? How or why is the Lord's Supper a sacrament?

2) Why do we share the meal as frequently or infrequently as we do?

3) What does 1 Corinthians 11:17-34 mean? What does it not mean?

4) Who prepares the meal? How does the pastor select people to assist with the distribution of the elements? What is done with the elements after the meal is over?

- There are four services of Word and Table in *The United Methodist Hymnal* on pages 6–31. Invite the group to study how the prayers are similar or dissimilar. (Each of the services uses a prayer called the Prayer of Great Thanksgiving. Note how the prayer is trinitarian in its format. That is, the first section rehearses the mighty acts of God the Father. The second section remembers the acts of Jesus Christ. The third section calls on the Holy Spirit to transform this meal into an act that reconciles us with God and with one another.)

- Invite the choir director, or someone who can read music or play a guitar or piano, to teach the group some of the Communion hymns in *The United Methodist Hymnal* (612–641). Ask if the congregation or the choir can sing one of these hymns the next time you share the meal of Holy Eucharist.

- Invite the group to watch the film *Babette's Feast*. This foreign film (dubbed or with English subtitles) offers a powerful artistic rendition of the transforming, reconciling power of the Lord's Supper. In the discussion afterward, note how a community at odds with one another and afraid of the meal is changed into a loving community that thoroughly enjoys the meal. Note, too, the central position played by the priest (the general) at the meal. What would have to happen for the sacrament of the Lord's Supper to have a similar effect on your congregation?

6. Remind the class to read Chapter 6 and its Scripture passages for the next class session. Be sure to designate someone in the class to offer the words of pardon when you next meet.

7. Conclude the class session by praying together the prayer of confession on pages 47 and 48. Remember to allow time for silent prayer and an examination of conscience. Then speak words of comfort that assure the class of God's love. End by inviting the class to say responsively:

LEADER: In the name of Jesus Christ, your sins are forgiven!

CLASS: In the name of Jesus Christ, your sins are forgiven, too!

Encourage the class to pass the peace with one another before they leave. If this is not a usual practice in your weekly worship, invite class members to offer a "kiss of peace" (a handshake or an embrace) to one another while saying, "I love you and I will pray for you this week."

If your congregation does not share the meal of Holy Eucharist on a weekly basis, ask your pastor to attend your class and share Communion with the class as an act of faith before you leave.

CHAPTER 6
Memory
(pp. 49–57)

1. Begin your class by praying the prayer on page 49 or by inviting one of the class members to offer his or her own prayer. Encourage the class to pray the printed prayer regularly throughout the week.

2. The primary purpose of this chapter is to understand that remembering is more than a mental act of calling to mind events that happened yesterday. It is a spiritual grace based in the resurrection of Jesus that enables the people and traditions of yesterday to bear witness to Christ today. It makes the past truly "present."

   The one act in which this is most true is the meal of Holy Eucharist. When we "do this in remembrance" of Jesus, it is not just a mental exercise in which we recall what Jesus once did. It is a recognition that God is making present in us the redeeming act of Christ *and* making mystically present around the Table again all the saints who have shared at the Table. God is re-membering the church body and making it whole. An excellent film rendition of this truth is the closing Communion scene in the movie *Places in the Heart*.

   As you make your lesson plans, decide whether you want to focus on memory as it relates to prophecy or as it relates to the communal life of the church.

3. If you choose to focus on memory as it relates to the act of prophecy, use the following questions to guide your discussion:
   • What is the difference between dwelling in the past and remembering the past? Which is more appropriate? Which does your church do? (If you need help in discerning how to move from living in the past to remembering the past, read Jeremiah 23:5-8, where the prophet declares that God's acts are always ongoing. Suggest that living in the past focuses our attention on ourselves, while remembering the past focuses our attention on God, who acts among us and within us.)
   • Do you know people whose testimony to the work of Christ in their lives is always about a long-past event and never about a recent work? Are these people remembering the past or escaping into the past? (Your church may struggle with the practice of baptismal reaffirmation. If this is the case, it may help to describe the act of reaffirming

our baptism as our attempt to bear witness to the ongoing work that Christ does in our lives to make us mature. It is similar to what we do when we profess in church one of the ancient creeds, such as the Apostles' Creed. It is one of the ways we recall a past event so that we may live faithfully in the present and the future.)

- If prophecy is not a matter of predicting the future but a way of remembering the past and judging the present in light of the faithful promises of God, how does that change your perception of the Old Testament prophets? What were the prophets doing when they proclaimed the word of the Lord?

- Why does the author suggest on pages 49 and 50 that much of what passes for prophecy today is really false prophecy? (It is concerned to predict what may happen tomorrow rather than remind people of God's covenantal promises.) Do you agree or disagree? Why?

- If the goal of history is *a person enfleshed* (Jesus) rather than *an event that is yet to occur*, does that build confidence in us as we prepare for the final judgment, or does it fill us with greater fear? Why?

4. If you choose to focus on memory as it relates to ways the church prepares for its communal life tomorrow, use the following questions to guide your discussion:

   - How is the story of the author's grandfather a parable of the church? (Life was restored through the recovery or remembrance of the tradition the grandfather had lived. Even though he had trouble accessing his memory, it had neither faded nor ceased to be. It was still there fully. He only needed someone to help him remember.) Who are the priests in your local church who help you remember God's faithful acts?

   - Why is the church today so quick to accept the culture's assumption that the adoption of new technologies will solve our woes? Why do we assume that the future of the church lies in "contemporary" worship that intentionally ignores the church's collected memory that we call tradition?

   - Is the church still the church if it doesn't retain its memory or tradition? Why? Why not?

   - Why does the church think that advertising campaigns are important? Does the church become more faithful by being more visible? Does increased attendance in the church mean that the gospel is being shared? What do advertisements in the telephone book or in the local newspaper tell the world about Jesus? Are there more faithful ways for the church to proclaim the gospel than through advertisements?

What happens to the church when it becomes a "product" we sell to consumers? What happens to the church when the marketing strategies used by business to manipulate audiences are given precedence over the faithful witness desired by God? (These are, of course, leading questions. They are designed to help the class push behind the ordinary rhetoric of the culture and hear God's call upon us.)

- Are there signs of God's gracious favor resting on the church today? If so, what are they? (Possible answers could focus on a variety of renewal movements, including *Walk to Emmaus*, *Covenant Discipleship*, DISCIPLE Bible study, and *Promise Keepers*.)
- Are there signs of God's anger resting on the church today? If so, what are they? What are some problem areas in the church that need to be addressed? How about in your local church? How could your local church become more faithful in these areas?

5. If there are those in the class who are ready to take additional steps in the formation of their faith, offer the following options:
    - Write a litany of thanksgiving that rehearses the mighty acts that God has performed on your behalf. Use Psalm 78 (or perhaps another psalm) as a guide. Begin with God's covenant with the people of Israel, work through both the New Testament witness in Jesus and the history of the church, and conclude with God's direction to and guidance of your local church today. Ask your pastor ahead of time if this litany could be used in worship some Sunday as a response to the sermon. (Depending on the shape the litany takes, it would be most appropriate for one of the Sundays in Easter or on All Saints' Sunday.)
    - Write a variation of the Prayer of Great Thanksgiving that you could use some Sunday when sharing the meal of Holy Eucharist. If your congregation has an annual homecoming celebration, this would be an excellent time to use the prayer in worship.
    - If your congregation has never written a church history, or if your present church history does not include the most recent generation of members, assemble a team to compose a list of the mighty acts that God has performed through your congregation. While collecting a list of pastors and chronicling the various building programs of the church is certainly important, be sure to include the individual testimonies and changed lives of the members in your church. Remembering the testimonies and sharing them with those who follow you will help bind together both past and future in the present. (If you select this option, be sure to send a copy of your finished history to your annual conference archives!)

6. Remind the class to read Chapter 7 and its accompanying Scripture passages for the next class session. Designate someone to pray the prayer of confession and offer the words of absolution.

   Since the next lesson is the final chapter in this book, be sure to come to your next class with a variety of options for your next study.

7. Conclude today's class by praying together the prayer of confession on page 57. Remember to allow time for silent prayer and an examination of conscience. Then speak words of comfort that assure the class of God's love. Invite the class to say responsively:

   LEADER: In the name of Jesus Christ, your sins are forgiven!

   CLASS: In the name of Jesus Christ, your sins are forgiven, too!

CHAPTER 7
Humility
(pp. 58–66)

1. Begin your class by praying the prayer on page 58 or by inviting one of the class members to offer his or her own prayer.

2. The purpose of this chapter is to face squarely the temptation of James and John, namely our propensity to see faith as an opportunity for personal glory (Mark 10:35-37) rather than as a call to be in humble service (Ephesians 2:10).

    Because Palm Sunday is often described in a way that presents a religion of glory rather than the victory of humility, care has been taken to focus attention on Luke's reconstruction of Jesus' entry. Instead of taking something away from Jesus, this focus actually reveals Jesus more clearly.

    Class members will be tempted in the discussion to focus solely on the alternative picture of Jesus' entry rather than upon the humility God wants to form within us. Be sure to spend some time on the reconstruction, but don't neglect the more weighty matter of humility!

3. The following questions may help the class explore the gift of humility:
    - If anyone is unclear about the references to Nike and Emmanuel on page 58, explain that *Nike* is the Greek word for "victory," while *Emmanuel* was the prophetic name meaning "God with us" that was given to Jesus. The point is that for Christians, what matters is not our own worldly success but God's faithful, divine presence.
    - Where did we learn that an upwardly-mobile lifestyle or an ever-increasing standard of living was a sign of God's blessing?
    - In light of Jesus' own downwardly-mobile lifestyle (see Philippians 2:5-11), how can we disciples live otherwise? Can we live differently from how our teacher did and still be, or claim to be, his disciples?
    - Do you know anyone who has turned his or her back on our culture's understanding of "the good life," choosing instead to be content with little? What role did faith play in his or her choice?
    - How does our baptismal call invite us to be humble? How does the meal of Holy Eucharist that we share weekly sustain our desire to go where Jesus leads? What have we given up or taken on to become a Christian?

- Why are we so prone to think about humility in a negative way as something to be avoided? How can it become something we view in a more positive light? (It was the path that Christ chose to live.)
- Respond to Luke's version of Jesus' entry into Jerusalem, as well as to the author's imaginative reconstruction of that event. Was the author's reconstruction believable? Why or why not? Was it more faithful to the life choices of Jesus than our traditional understanding of the "triumphal" entry? Why or why not? How would you describe Jesus' entry into Jerusalem?
- Has your understanding of Jesus or of the Christian faith changed as a result of reading this chapter?

4. If there are those in the class who are ready to take additional steps in the formation of their faith, offer the following options:
   - Serve a person or a group of people who cannot or will not give you anything in return. Contact your annual conference office and find out when the next training seminar will be offered for people interested in visiting either an inmate on death row or a surviving victim of a violent crime. Work in a soup kitchen, a union mission, or a homeless shelter. Provide free custodial help at your church, volunteer to answer the phones, or mow the grass during the summer. Do something that will not offer you any recognition. Do something that requires that you learn to be humble.
   - Invite your pastor, or take the time to prepare yourself, to lead your class in either a weekend retreat or a multiple-week study of spiritual gifts. By discovering what our gifts are, we can become more intentional about being a humble people, ready to take our rightful place in the one body of Christ.

5. Allow ample time toward the end of the class session for members of the class to share how God, through this study, has begun to change who they are and how they think about the Christian faith. Ask if they have any lingering questions or concerns that need to be addressed.

6. Conclude the class session by praying together the prayer of confession on pages 65 and 66. Remember to allow time for silent prayer and an examination of conscience. Then speak words of comfort that assure the class of God's love. Invite the class to say responsively:
LEADER: In the name of Jesus Christ, your sins are forgiven!
CLASS: In the name of Jesus Christ, your sins are forgiven, too!

7. Thank the members of the class for taking the readings seriously and

for joining in the discussions as readily as they did. If you have not alerted the class to this study guide at the back of the book, do so now. If you have not made your class aware of the options for continuing their Christian formation that are included in each chapter's study guide, show them where to find these options. Encourage interested class members to covenant with one another to take one or more of these steps of Christian formation.

As a final act of faith, invite the class to stand and join hands while you offer a prayer of thanksgiving to God for guiding your class so graciously.

For Further Study

The following resources for congregations, pastors, and teachers will help pilgrims continue their faithful walk with Jesus.

BIBLE STUDY

The NIV Study Bible: Tenth Anniversary Edition, Zondervan Publishing House, 1995.

COVENANT DISCIPLESHIP

Covenant Discipleship: Christian Formation Through Mutual Accountability, by David Lowes Watson; Discipleship Resources, 1991.

Class Leaders: Recovering a Tradition, by David Lowes Watson; Discipleship Resources, 1991.

Forming Christian Disciples: The Role of Covenant Discipleship and Class Leaders in the Congregation, by David Lowes Watson; Discipleship Resources, 1991.

MAKING DISCIPLES AND MENTORING

Come to the Waters: Baptism & Our Ministry of Welcoming Seekers & Making Disciples, by Daniel T. Benedict, Jr.; Discipleship Resources, 1996.

Gracious Voices: Shouts and Whispers for God Seekers, compiled and edited by William P. McDonald; Discipleship Resources, 1996.

By Water and the Spirit: Making Connections for Identity and Ministry, by Gayle Felton; Discipleship Resources, 1997.

Echoing the Word: The Ministry of Forming Disciples, by Grant S. Sperry-White; Discipleship Resources, 1998.

Accompanying the Journey: A Handbook for Sponsors, by Lester Ruth; Discipleship Resources, 1997.

PRAYER AND SPIRITUAL DISCIPLINES

Prayer: Finding the Heart's True Home, by Richard J. Foster; Harper San Francisco, 1992.

Celebration of Discipline: The Path to Spiritual Growth, by Richard J. Foster; Harper San Francisco, 1988.

Soul Feast: An Invitation to the Christian Spiritual Life, by Marjorie J. Thompson; Westminster John Knox Press, 1995.

SACRAMENTS

Remember Who You Are: Baptism, A Model for Christian Life, by William H. Willimon; The Upper Room, 1980.

Sunday Dinner: The Lord's Supper and the Christian Life, by William H. Willimon; The Upper Room, 1981.

WORSHIP

United Methodist Worship, by Hoyt L. Hickman; Abingdon Press, 1991.